EARLY AMERICAN
FIREPLACES

EARLY AMERICAN FIREPLACES

by

PAUL R. LADD

HASTINGS HOUSE   *Publishers*   New York

Library of Congress Cataloging in Publication Data

Ladd, Paul Revere, 1894–
  Early American fireplaces.

  Bibliography: p.
  Includes index.
  1. Fireplaces—United States—History. I. Title.
TH7425.L3 1977   697'.1'0973   77–865
ISBN 0–8038–1930–7

Published simultaneously in Canada by
Saunders of Toronto, Ltd., Don Mills, Ontario

Printed in the United States of America
Designed by Al Lichtenberg

*This book is affectionately dedicated
to my wife Helen Douglas Ladd,
with whom I have enjoyed the
flickering light and the warmth of a fireplace
on countless evenings in over
fifty years of married life.*

WINDMILL COTTAGE
East Greenwich, Rhode Island

This fireplace in Windmill Cottage is one of six around a central chimney, but it is the one which has seen the real activity in the house. Once owned by Henry Wadsworth Longfellow, the great American poet, the house has been the property of the author and his wife for the last thirty-five years.

Longfellow gave the house and also the Windmill, which he purchased, had moved and joined to the house, to his lifelong friend, George Washington Greene and his family.

The fireplace, which once cooked food and baked bread for the occupants, has been the scene of special events, including a wedding about which Maud Howe Eliot wrote to Mr. Ladd as follows:

I attended the wedding of Rev. Brenton Greene to his cousin Katherine Greene. I was accompanied to this wedding at Windmill Cottage by my mother, Julia Ward Howe, and sitting around the fireplace with them were Charles Sumner, George Washington Greene, Henry W. Longfellow and my uncle, Sam Ward.

The house or cottage of Windmill Cottage was built around 1790. The Windmill has no date but was grinding grain during the Revolution. The views shown here and on page ten were taken during Christmas holidays of two different years.

CONTENTS

FOREWORD

In this delightful book, the product of years of collecting and study, Paul R. Ladd has done more than painstakingly enumerate and describe the fireplace equipment used when household heating and cooking depended entirely on the fireplaces clustered around a great stone or brick chimney. He quietly leads us to the hearths of early America and there proceeds to explain the all embracing importance of the kitchen fireplace in an existence still without stoves and when electricity and gas played no part in daily life.

Here the many ramifications of the story of the fireplace are unfolded. We are introduced to the process of building the chimney. We go to the brick kiln for bricks and brickmaking and watch the bricklayer at work. We learn the roles that the charcoal pit, the iron furnace and foundry, and the rolling and slitting mills play in producing equipment for the fireplace. We follow the evolution of oven construction and are faced with the constant need for firewood. We learn the names of the fireplace features together with the many fireplace tools, utensils and accessories and how they are used. We gain an insight into the manifold functions of the fireplace as it served for cooking, for illumination, for its part in making indigo dye, for candlemaking and for pewter casting. We learn how the wood ashes were stored, collected and then used for the potash that among other things, was required for soapmaking, hulling corn and for making pearlash for baking powder.

Above all we almost take part ourselves in this now gone existence when the kitchen fireplace was the working heart of the house. We are brought into its immediate orbit, with its warmth and cheer, where not only the working activities of family and friends were centered, but their social life as well.

Mr. Ladd has drawn on his studious interest and knowledge acquired through years of collecting the homely objects of the past to produce a rewarding and illuminating book.

Mrs. Antoinette F. Downing
Rhode Island Commission
on Preservation of Historic Buildings

Christmas Time at Windmill Cottage—Author's Home.

ACKNOWLEDGMENTS

When this volume was undertaken, I had little realization of the ramifications of the subject, and what a full treatment involved. Nor did I realize how many books and articles I would consult and how many museums, historic homes and historical societies I would need to visit or contact. All of this was in spite of, and because of, my long interest in fireplaces and having been a collector of heating and lighting devices for many years.

It is, therefore, with all the more sincerity and gratitude that I extend my warmest thanks to the librarians, authors, antiquarians, directors, curators and other museum personnel, photographers, and interested individuals, who have assisted me generously with advice, information or material.

Among the many who have rendered assistance in the preparation of this book, there are some persons who deserve individual mention and I trust that I omit no one to whom I am thus especially indebted.

Noel P. Conlon, Research Associate, Rhode Island Historical Society

Mrs. Antoinette Downing, Consultant, Providence Preservation Society and Chairman, R. I. Historical Preservation Commission

Leonard Panaggio, Rhode Island Development Council

William C. Warren, Director and Joseph S. Van Why, Curator, Stowe-Day Foundation

Herbert C. Darbee, Executive Secretary, Connecticut Historical Commission

Alexander J. Wall, President, Old Sturbridge Village

Robert Farrell, Varnum Continentals

Mrs. Gordon MacLeod, President, Gilbert Stuart Association

Mrs. William Roelker, Jr., owner, Governor William Greene birthplace

William Foster, editor, *The Pendulum*, East Greenwich, Rhode Island

Mrs. Joseph Greene, Cocumscussoc Association

Bertram K. Little, former Director, Society for the Preservation of New England Antiquities

Mrs. Charles H. Watkins, owner, Captain Andrew Fuller House, Middleton, Massachusetts

Mrs. Anne Crawford Allen Holst, antiquarian, lecturer

Mrs. Gilbert L. Bean, Sylvanus Thayer House, Braintree Historical Association

Joseph T. Butler, Curator, Sleepy Hollow Restoration, Tarrytown

Frank L. Horton, Old Salem, Inc., Winston-Salem, North Carolina

Mrs. Albert Harkness, former Regent, Mt. Vernon Ladies Association of the Union

Robert D. Burhans, Director, Kenmore, Fredericksburg, Virginia

Edwin B. Rollins, Professor Emeritus, Tufts College

Nancy Richards, Museum Director, Concord Antiquarian Society

Grace McAuslan, a librarian, Providence Atheneum

Martha McPartland, Librarian, East Greenwich Free Library

Paul R. Ladd, Jr., photographer, author and teacher

Dorothy A. Freeman, Pioneer Village, City of Salem, Massachusetts

Edward Durell, Durell Museum; President, Union Fork and Hoe Co.

Thomas H. deValcourt, Curator, The Longfellow House, Cambridge

Mrs. Arthur C. Hitchcock, owner; Hitchcock House, Putney, Vermont

Raymond E. Townsend, Colonial Williamsburg; former editor, *The Chronicle of E.A.I.A.*

Mrs. Rose T. Briggs, Curator, Plymouth Antiquarian Society

Carl A. Johnson, Executive Vice President, Strawbery Banke, Inc.

Mrs. Lawrence Moore, Saxtons River, Vermont

Miss Nancy Sibley Wilkins, owner of Joshua George Homestead, Warner, N. H.

Amos G. Avery, owner of Avery Homestead, Ledyard, Conn.

I. E. Liverant, owner of Liverant House, Colchester, Conn.

Robert Avery Smith, Antiquarian, and owner of Jehiel Webb House, Rockingham, Vermont

Mrs. Dana Parks, Jr., Asst. to Director, New Hampshire Historical Society

Robert Davis, owner, Capt. John Knap House, Stamford, Connecticut

Mrs. John M. Hudock, Regent, Putnam Hill Chapter D.A.R., Greenwich, Connecticut

INTRODUCTION

A telephone call from Old Sturbridge Village to my retreat in New Hampshire carried a request that I speak at their Antique Collectors Week End program on "The Hearth, Its Uses and Utensils." To be sure, I had collected fireplace utensils along with lighting devices for some years. Moreover, I had taken photographs in the form of color slides of the major part of my extensive collection.

I accepted the invitation and began to read up on the subject. I was surprised to find that, as important as the fireplace was to Early America, no book or account that I could find treated the subject as a whole. There were chapters here and there which described and illustrated the fireplace, but such chapters were in books on The Early American Home, Colonial Days, The Architecture of Houses, or Furniture Treasury or some such broader subject. And yet when I began to study and do research on the subject of the fireplace itself I found that the Early American Fireplace was an institution, a broad based subject with many ramifications.

There has always been an appreciation of the fireplace but there seems to have been all too little recognition of its importance as a dominant factor in the lives of our ancestors. The colonists in America depended upon the fireplace for light, for warmth, for the heat to do their cooking, and for the means to do many household crafts such as candle making, dyeing and soap making.

Moreover, I began to realize that the fireplace, no matter how essential, just did not appear as if by magic. Materials and workmanship were required for its construction, following which a plentiful supply of wood had to be available. This is why a separate though limited treatment is given to the charcoal pit, the brick kiln, the bricklayer and the forest.

The early American household, for everyday use of the fireplace, needed a full complement of "pots and kittles". This brings into focus the iron works, which includes the charcoal pit, the foundry and the forge, and, of course, the blacksmith.

In addition to its functions as a source of light and heat the fireplace became the social center of the family, a place for the women to spin and gossip, and for the men to whittle, to tell "yarns," and to relax, if ever our forebears had time to relax. This important attribute of the fireplace I do not intend to neglect.

The fireplace produced an important and useful by-product in the form of wood ashes which had an economic value as potash for fertilizer, for soap making, and for the manufacture of pearlash. The potash or ashery therefore, is the subject of another short chapter of this volume. A chapter giving some old recipes important in early fireplace cookery is also included.

The oven was usually an integral part of the early fireplace. It is called the bake or brick oven, and along with the fireplace itself, the oven went through a change, principally of location. As the oven changed its position from behind the fire "box" to the side or cheek of the chimney place and then outside, so too did the fireplace itself change, especially in size. The subject of the development of the oven and fireplace has a special place as does that of the tools and utensils which were used in and around it.

When I refer to the Early American Fireplace I mean the principal or central fireplace, frequently called the kitchen or keeping room fireplace, which is the subject of this book. Among the earliest settlers of America this was the only fireplace, for the reason that there was only one, or at most two rooms which constituted the home.

As affluence spread and as houses became larger with a number of rooms and ofttimes an upper floor, small fireplaces were built into the parlor room and the chambers. Such fireplaces were frequently constructed as part of a central chimney, and appeared especially in the towns and "cities." They were built primarily for warmth, although they were used frequently to heat water or for some light chore. These minor fireplaces were often surrounded with beautiful paneling or sheathing and some have very decorative mantels.

I have included with the fireplace illustrations several of this type, but I am not dwelling upon them. Though there is an almost endless variety of architectural treatment in their construction and decoration, they did not have the multiple uses, nor did they supply the essential needs, nor were they the social center or the very life of the family as was the case with the "kitchen" fireplace.

To continue with the story of the writing of this book, after I spoke on fireplaces at Old Sturbridge Village, I prepared an article on Early Rhode Island Fireplaces at the request of the Rhode Island Historical Society. I next included the New England area in an address on Fireplaces to members of the Rushlight Club, after which it was published in their Bulletin.

After these ventures in the fireplace field, it did not take much encouragement to consider the preparation of a book on the subject, although in the beginning I had little idea of the ramifications and the enlargement of the subject which was required to have anything near a complete story on the Early Fireplace.

There are many persons who, today, enjoy an early fireplace in an old home, but probably there are few who have had to put to use a fireplace for practical living as the author and his wife have had to do. I had had an interest in fireplaces for many years and have collected fireplace utensils. Besides, my wife and I have never been without a fireplace—one or more—during our married life. There are six fireplaces in our 1790 home of the last forty years, and there are two fireplaces in our "summer" residence.

The 1938 hurricane which swept the East Coast left our house without electricity, which was not restored for a full month. We called upon our extensive fireplace utensil collection, and used the devices necessary to cook our meals. We also got our entire warmth from the fireplace during this period. In this manner we managed, with candles for light, much as our ancestors had to do in the days of long ago. The fireplace, which cooked our food and warmed our bodies, also refreshed our spirits.

PART I

The
Early American
Fireplace

The author's restored fireplace at his "summer" retreat in New Hampshire. Note the ceiling hooks still in place.

Ceiling hooks extending into the room in front of the fireplace. The hooks are arranged so that poles or rods can be inserted in a position parallel to the face of the fireplace. In such a manner, many things could be dried, from herbs to fruits and vegetables, to clothing.

THE FIREPLACE:
ITS SERVICES AND USES

The Early American fireplace had uses which are little realized by the descendants of the settlers of America. Today we enjoy an open fire but we have no dependence upon it.

One of the primary functions of the early fireplace was for warmth. The colonists lived a rugged life especially in winter, and the heat of the fireplace, even with its limitations helped them to survive. On a bitter cold night water would freeze when not too far from the hearth, and when the fire had to be kept blazing during the night, members of the family would take turns to watch and stoke the fire.

Another most important use of the fireplace was for cooking. Utensils were required for preparing the family meals and in the first years in the colonies, pots and kettles had to be brought to America in sailing ships from the mother country. It was not long, however, before iron was found and worked in the new country. The first cast iron pot, a small one, was manufactured at the Saugus, Massachusetts, ironworks which used the name "Company of Undertakers for the Iron Works in New England."

The log cabins of early settlers were dark even in the daytime, and the light from the fireplace was the only light to be had until candles could supplement the firelight. To get the maximum light when needed, pine faggots would be tossed on the burning logs from time to time. Tallow was scarce at first and imported candles were expensive. As time went on, however, a number of lighting devices were put to use which could burn fuel such as grease or fish oil. These devices which were used in and around the fireplace during Colonial days are described in a chapter on illumination.

Lesser uses or services of the fireplace were many, as the heat of the fire dried clothes, herbs and certain of the fruits and vegetables. The chimneys of a few fireplaces were constructed with a vent to trap some of the

17

smoke, with which hams were smoked in an inside "smoke house" or pocket room off the chimney. There are a few examples also of the smoke and hot air from the fire being used to turn a smoke jack. The rotation of the vanes of a smoke jack in the chimney was transferred to the spit by means of a chain.

The fireplace was the source of hot coals or embers which were used for lighting pipes, to put in warming pans and foot warmers, or to supply the needs of neighbors whose fire had gone out. The ashes of the hard woods such as oak, maple and hickory were a valuable product of the fireplace, and they were kept for home use and sometimes sold. From the ashes lye was extracted for use in soap making. The potash in ashes was a fertilizer. Pearlash, later known as saleratus, was also obtained and used in baking.

We might consider the fireplace to have been cluttered with utensils. They had to be kept handy, and often there was nowhere else to put them, especially in the very early one room house which was the keeping room as well as the kitchen-living room. Even shelves and cupboards were scarce. The houses which were built with several rooms and particularly those with a pantry, must have delighted the housewife by providing a place to store kitchen furnishings which were not used regularly.

Besides being a limited depository or storehouse, the hearth and the area around the fireplace was used for those household crafts and chores which demanded heat for hot water, or for warmth of the person. Milk was heated in cheese making, tallow was melted for molding or dipping candles, lye with fats was boiled in soap making, the indigo dye was kept warm in a pot by the fire, and the warmth of the fire was a blessing to the housewife when she was spinning or weaving in the cold months.

A niche or spot near the fireplace kept powder, the tinder box and tobacco dry, and firearms were frequently on the lintel or above it as a central and convenient place in case of emergency. Nowadays there are two schools of thought and action as regards the best display of old fireplace utensils. Some exhibits try to show everything possible related to the fireplace. This really clutters the area, but the various implements can be seen. Other exhibits are more restrained and show only a relatively few of the more important utensils, while additional ones may be put in another small room or pantry if there is one. There is good reasoning behind each method of arrangement.

DEVELOPMENT OF THE FIREPLACE AND OVEN

One might think that the fireplace and the oven were static features of the Early American Home. However, they have gone through a process of development or evolution. The changing "architecture" of the fireplace and the brick oven has been touched upon elsewhere, but there needs to be some elaboration because of the importance of the changes in the matter of heating efficiency, convenience and safety.

The brick masons in the early days were not engineers, nor technicians, nor architects, but they knew from experience how to build a fireplace. Nevertheless, judging from the records, there must have been many fireplaces which would not draw properly. The author remembers well when he had a fireplace restored by a New Hampshire native bricklayer. The author was to be away at the time and left explicit directions: the fireplace sides were to be splayed and there were to be two layers of brick showing between the lintel and the mantel. When the author re-

turned, the fireplace was finished, to be sure, but not in accordance with directions. When the brick mason was asked, "why?" the answer came back, "Well, it draws, don't it?" This, to the workman, was the one and only requisite of a fireplace.

The author had the good fortune to see an original "fireplace" hearth at Penshurst in England. It was an open hearth of stone in the center of a great hall. On the hearth was an iron bar supported by an upright at each end, a sort of double or joined andirons. On each side of the bar, wood was leaned at about a 60-degree angle, in readiness to be lighted. There was no chimney, just a high ceiling, and the smoke from the fire would eventually go out of the room through a hole in the roof, or from under the eaves or even through open doors.

Our early colonists at first had to settle for just such a fireplace, the open hearth, for a decade at least. A hole or flue through the roof was the first development. Then a chimney was built around the hole to give draught and to provide some protection from the elements, however meager. Following this the chimney was brought down inside the room and above the fire. Still later the chimney of brick or stone was made to enclose the fire except for a front opening. This now constituted what today we term a fireplace.

In many cases the fireplace remained in the center of the room, but fireplaces were increasingly built against or as part of the outside wall itself. When the Governor William Greene house was built (see illustration in Part II) the chimney took up the entire wall on one side of the two room house.

Chimneys were built of wood in some of the first homes of the New England colonists, and together with a thatched roof, a real fire hazard existed. A report in the *Boston Gazette* of February 19, 1754 reads,

WOODEN CHIMNEY. A small house about seven miles from Annapolis, Maryland, which had a wooden chimney took fire while the occupants were away and burned down.

Wooden chimneys were such a fire hazard that they were prohibited in some of the colonies. When Washington, as President, made a tour of the Eastern States, he found it worthy of note in his diary that dwellings generally had stone or brick chimneys.

The most dramatic changes in fireplace development took place before the colonists came to America. In the first primitive shelters erected in this country, however, the fireplace took on some of its more ancient aspects, and went through much the same evolution.

Mrs. Antoinette Downing in her book, *Early Homes of Rhode Island* wrote,

A great stone chimney, the distinctive feature of the northern Rhode Island houses, formed an entire end wall. The great stone fireplace was wide enough and high enough, to sit in, on a winter's evening.

There was good reason to have large fireplaces, and the smoke, when it did smoke, had to be endured. The fireplace did yeoman service and size was required for the cooking, heating and all the necessary uses of the fire and the firelight. In addition, the bake oven occupied space in the chimney place, and there had to be room enough to operate this facility also.

The large fireplace could accommodate huge logs which extended for most of its width and spread out the fire over a larger area. Although considerable warmth was felt in the room, the greater part of the heat was lost up the huge chimney.

The brick oven played a part in the next evolution of the fireplace, which was one of size. It will be noted that some of the very early fireplaces have the bake oven in the back wall of the chimney place, and even in the center of this wall. The bake oven was more often located at one side or the other, however. This position of the oven no doubt came about in order that the fire which was built in the oven to heat the bricks or stone could use the chimney flue. The smoke and gases curved around in the oven, came out the opening and were drawn up the chimney. There were distinct disadvantages in this location of the oven, however, which included the problem of access and the matter of safety from the flames.

I am not excluding the fact that there were outside ovens even in the North, but these were few and they were as likely as not built against or connected with the chimney. Of course we are familiar with the Southern plantation fireplaces which were in the outbuildings. A shift in the location of the oven from the back wall to the side wall still enabled the oven fire to make use of the regular chimney flue. A recessed shelf at the corner or front side of the brickwork would be deep enough for the smoke to pass out of the door and up through the overhanging flue.

An ash pit was generally placed beneath the oven in this type of arrangement. This was also the case in the next type of oven which had a flue of its own, or an inside flue.

BARONS HALL
Penshurst Place, Kent, England

An original open-hearth fireplace.

This type was built so that the door generally was flush with the brickwork at one side or the other of the fireplace opening. Finally, but at a much later date, a fire box was constructed underneath the oven with the heat circulating around but mostly concentrating on the bottom bricks of the oven.

The fireplace photographs show the brick or bake ovens in their different locations. With the latter day location of the oven in the face of the brickwork outside of the fireplace itself, there was less need of a huge fireplace. Therefore, along with this change requiring considerable brickwork at the right or left of the fire "box," the size of the fireplace was automatically or purposely reduced. The narrower fireplace opening actually brought about greater heat for the room as a narrower chimney throat required less draught and therefore less loss of heat.

These experiments to solve the problem of smoky chimneys show that the size of the fireplace and chimney throat had much to do with smoke nuisance.

A Paris physician, Louis Savot, in the 16th century was perhaps the first to make a scientific study of smoky chimneys. He did not correct the real trouble, but he improved the form by narrowing the width of the fireplace and thus reducing the air which could enter on each side of the fire.

Benjamin Franklin was troubled by smoky chimneys and often spoke of the disadvantages of a large fireplace. In 1745 he wrote,

> They almost always smoke if the door be not left open, the cold air so nips the backs and heels of those that set before the fire that they have no comfort

He added that even without the discomfort caused by smoke:

> A man is scorched before while he is froze behind.

Franklin did something about his pet peeve. He designed the stove that still bears his name.

Count Rumford in the late 18th century devoted time and talent to cure smoking chimneys. He wrote,

> I have never been obliged (except once) to have recourse to any other method of cure than merely reducing the fireplace and throat of the chimney, or that part of it which lies immediately above the fireplace to a proper form and just dimensions.

It was not long in the Colonial period before well constructed, durable and fine appearing homes were built, with upper floors to be heated. The central chimney became a feature of the home. The foundation of this chimney reached down into the basement or below frost level if there were no basement. The kitchen fireplace maintained its accustomed place on the first floor and was the largest fireplace of all. The narrow stairway which very often was opposite the front door occupied the space on one side of the great chimney which might otherwise have been a fireplace. This left two sides of the chimney for two fireplaces besides the kitchen fireplace.

The homes with such a central chimney were built around the chimney so that the parlor, sitting room and upstairs chambers could have small fireplaces. The home of the author has such a chimney, around which are six fireplaces. Fireplaces also have been built, but are not usual, in the basement or attic of a large house. It is regrettable that many central chimney fireplaces were entirely dismantled when they were superseded by stoves, but it is fortunate in other cases that they were simply covered over, making complete restoration by descendents or Historical Societies unnecessary.

Many old homes with handsome fireplaces have been destroyed by fire, and many have been in the "path of progress" and destroyed, but those which remain are becoming more and more appreciated and preserved, frequently by Historical and Preservation Societies when they pass out of private hands. A letter to the author from Prof. Edwin B.

Rollins sums up the evolution of the fireplace:

84 Packard Avenue
Somerville, Mass.

Dear Mr. Ladd:

It was a real privilege to be able to attend the Rushlight Club meeting and hear your interesting and informative talk on fireplaces. For years we visited many old houses and the fireplaces always interested me. There were big ones with room for an "ingle nook" and the little chamber fireplaces hardly larger than a Franklin stove.

The fire in the center of the floor of the great room, or hall, of the castle appears to have been the first attempt to warm a large interior and probably was not much more effective than gathering around a bonfire out of doors. But people were more hardy then.

The inconvenience of smoke from the central fire is said to have led to building the fire against a wall and providing just above it an opening to a flue which, if the draft was strong, probably carried off some of the smoke. It could not have been long before someone added a hood to capture all the smoke. To push the fire into a hole made in the wall and connect with a flue produced the true fireplace.

In an old house in Newburyport I saw a small fireplace occupying one corner of a room like a corner cupboard. The opening was not at floor level but raised to a convenient height.

On one visit my attention was called to a niche, either in the fireplace wall or nearby where the tinder box was kept. Tinder must be very dry in order to ignite readily from a tiny spark and how could it be better kept so than in contact with continually warm masonry?

The marble-front fireplace was a form fairly common in fine houses of my boyhood days. I think there was usually a grate for burning coal rather than wood which might smoke up the mantel.

The small open fireplace with a grate for coal sometimes had a sort of shelf adjacent to the fire where food could be kept warm. This was called a "hob." Dickens, in the Christmas Carol, has Bob Cratchit compound a hot mixture in a jug and, "put it on the hob to simmer."

Add a fender to the fireplace and its development is complete. It also tended to keep the rest of the hearth neat.

Sincerely,
Edwin B. Rollins

Dating the Evolution of the Fireplace and Oven

A rough dating of Early American Fireplaces can be approximated as a result of study and examination of early houses, their fireplaces and their ovens. The author, who has personally visited and inspected many such historic houses and their fireplaces, submits this period classification:

Early 17th Century: Large and moderate size fireplaces with no oven built in. Baking was done on and before the fire by pots (Dutch ovens) and reflector ovens, respectively. A large fire or several lesser fires could be contained in the fireplace for separate cooking.

Middle and Late 17th Century: The fireplaces were still large. An oven of stone or brick was built into the back wall of the fireplace. There was no separate flue. The great chimney served as the oven flue also.

Early 18th Century: The fireplace was still large. Around 1720 the oven began to appear in the side wall, or in a recessed corner of the side wall. The great chimney still served the oven fire as a flue.

Middle and Late 18th Century: Around 1750 and later, the oven began to be built in the outside or face of the fireplace either on the left or the right side. This construction

23

Bake oven from Captain John Knap House. A close-up of the fieldstone, primitive, oven in the back wall of the keeping room fireplace of the Captain John Knap House in Stamford, Connecticut—now the home of Robert Davis. *Courtesy of Robert Davis.*

required a separate flue for the oven, which flue was located in the middle of the oven space or in the front part of the opening behind the removable door. The fireplace now had less need of great size because the baking was done on the exterior.

With the advent of the oven on the face of the fireplace, an open box-like pit appeared below the oven for the storage of ashes. Shortly before the stove replaced the fireplace for family cooking, a fire box below the oven was used occasionally to heat the underside of the oven above instead of building a fire in the oven itself. This method was not overly successful.

As stated above, the period designation of different types of fireplaces and ovens in early America is anything but hard and fast. There was much overlapping for good and sundry reasons, but the dating is provided for those who are interested in this aspect of fireplace construction.

FIREPLACE TERMINOLOGY

Generally everyone knows what a fireplace is, but not everyone knows the names of the areas or parts which make up the total entity. To some, the hearth is synonymous with the fireplace, and in common cognizance this may be so. Yet there is much more to the fireplace than the hearth. The dictionary defines "hearth" as the floor of the fireplace, while the fireplace is defined as "a recess or structure in or on which a fire is built, especially the part of the chimney which opens into a room."

There are other parts of the fireplace:

The Lintel is the horizontal support for bricks or stone over the opening. In many of the early fireplaces the lintel was made of a huge, squared oak beam which stretched across the top of the opening. On occasion we find a stone lintel of granite, while in a later period a flat iron bar gave the necessary support. The lintel has also been called the *chimney girt* (for girder).

The Manteltree: a little used, chiefly architectural term for the wooden beam or arch forming the lintel of a fireplace.

The Chimney Place: another name for the fireplace with its hearth and opening in which the fire is built.

The Chimney Piece or Overmantel is the wall space, sometimes paneled or decorated, between the lintel and/or mantelpiece and the ceiling.

The Jamb: there are two jambs, which are the vertical pieces or parts forming the front at each side of the fireplace opening. Sometimes the jamb is wood over brick or stone, and sometimes the brick or stone is bare. Very often the jambs are an integral part of the mantel, especially in the chamber or parlor fireplaces.

The Jamb Hook: a partial ring or hook inserted in a jamb to hold fireplace tools such as tongs, shovel, and poker.

Splayed Sides: the early fireplace had sides which were usually splayed outward from the back wall to the front opening, but sometimes other shapes were used. In some 17th century Rhode Island fireplaces of stone the sides were splayed. But when brick was introduced the sides and even the back were rounded, as can be seen in the James Greene House and the Wanton-Lyman-Hazard House.

The Mantel: the plain or ornamented structure above a fireplace usually having a shelf or projecting ledge. The mantel is not so much a feature of the earliest kitchen fireplaces as it is of the parlor and chamber types.

The Mantelpiece: a projection or shelf which runs the length of and above the lintel. Occasionally a narrow shelf over the early kitchen fireplace was brought about by the placing of the lintel. In common usage, the term is interchangeable with the mantel.

The Inglenook: a corner or side space where a person could sit or even stand upright in the fireplace.

The Hob: a projection or shelf at the back or side of the fireplace.

The Chimney Nook: a place in the chimney for holding or hiding small treasures or materials which needed to be kept dry.

The Scullery: a chimney place or fireplace used for the rough and dirty work of the kitchen. Also the place where the kitchen utensils were cleaned and kept. This kind of work usually had to be done in the one kitchen fireplace, but occasionally there were two adjoining fireplaces, one of which was the scullery. Sometimes the scullery fireplace was on another level—in the cellar or basement room if there was one.

The Brick or Bake Oven: a baking oven originally built into the back or side brickwork of the chimney place or in the brickwork outside of the fireplace opening at either side. The brick oven has been erroneously called a Dutch oven (which is an iron utensil). Some ovens were built in the shape of a dome and called "beehive" ovens, a style which is now quite rare. Below the oven opening was an ash pit in which the wood ash drawn out of the oven could be stored.

Luting was that part of the baking process which involved sealing the brick oven door after the food had been put inside. Oak leaves were gathered in the fall and kept on hand to put under bread loaves or cakes when placed in the oven to keep them clean.

BRICKS AND BRICKLAYERS

As I pointed out earlier, the very earliest settlers resorted to chimneys built of wood and clay which were a fire hazard and such wood construction was soon abandoned or prohibited. Stone was abundant and was used for chimneys and the fireplace quite extensively before bricks were made and bricklayers became available. Before long, granite was quarried and used as a hearth and for the lintel as well as in the fireplace walls. This is particularly noticeable in the Connecticut area.

Brick, however, became the mainstay of chimney construction in a relatively short time because of its greater flexibility and greater ease in handling. In order to manufacture bricks, a source of clay, an abundant supply of firewood for running a kiln, and plenty of water were necessities. Also, the know-how of molding and of burning the bricks was needed. Lime for use as a mortar in laying bricks was first obtained by crushing or grinding oyster shells, following which limestone was obtained from quarries.

There were bricklayers among the early settlers. In fact, they were here and ready even before the materials became available. Bricklayers were among the first arrivals in Jamestown. In 1656, William White of Boston, a bricklayer, was in Providence, and by order of the town he was to be accommodated with a house lot. Two years later a share of meadow was granted to him. He apparently found little opportunity to follow his trade, for it was not until 1698 that bricks were mentioned in any Providence records.

Among the first of the tradesmen to arrive at the settlement of Salem (Massachusetts) was a man skilled in brickmaking. According to the writings of Rev. Francis Higginson, a brick mixer and brick kiln were set up in 1629, but little could be accomplished in construction because of the scarcity of lime for mortar. The settlers in New Amsterdam in 1626 found clay, oyster shells for lime, plenty of wood for burning, but lacked experienced workmen.

Elsewhere in the Colonies, brick making

Old bricks which make the walls of a smoke house behind the chimney of a fireplace in the Lillibridge House, East Greenwich, R.I.

was encouraged. Haverhill granted ¾ of an acre and clay pits to John Hoitt in 1650, Maine was making bricks in 1674, and Philadelphia had brickmakers in 1690. However, before there was a plentiful supply of bricks in the Colonies, many were brought over from England as ballast in the ships. Marion Nicholl Rawson wrote that she gives little credence to any great amount of bricks brought on ships as ballast, because as she said, "Stones cost nothing," and yet there was good reason to use brick, if available. Francis Higginson brought over ten thousand bricks in the same year that the brick mixer was set up in Salem.

According to the Pioneer Village exhibit in Salem,

The brick mixer had the appearance of a crude cement mixer. Clay was plentiful and was placed in the mixer and mixed with water by means of flails turned by horse power. The horse was hitched to a long beam and led around the mixer. As the massive arm turned the spike-studded shaft, the ingredients became thoroughly mixed and flowed smoothly from an opening at the floor of the machine onto a molding platform whose wooden forms were filled and left in the sun to dry. The bricks were then kiln baked with wood fires.

In a large number of the settlements the early bricks were all made by hand, the workman dusting the mold with sand and then packing it with soft clay. When hardened somewhat the bricks were dumped from the mold onto a level floor and dried in the sun.

After a "sun bath," the bricks were stacked in the shape of arches. Wood for burning was put in the arches to complete the kiln.

Noah Webster asked a friend named Pickering for a brick making recipe and received the following instructions.

That molds be shod with iron, that each mold be for a single brick, that they should be thrown into a tub of fine sifted dust to prevent the bricks from sticking to the sides, that the mixing of clay and water might be done in various ways to get the proper consistency. The burning of bricks took from two days to a week. The fire box of the kiln is made of the bricks themselves.

Mr. Pickering said that in some process bricks were cut instead of molded. He said that the end of a brick is called the "header", the long side a "stretcher."

The author has a double brick mold which was used when bricks were done by hand. This mold was from the old home of Robert Reese in West Virginia, in which the bricks for that house were made.

Through the courtesy of Nancy Richards, Museum Director of the Concord Antiquarian Society, excerpts for the period of the year 1795 from an account book of Ithamar Spaulding seem to be of sufficient interest with which to conclude this subject. Mr. Spaulding was a stone cutter who turned part time bricklayer.

A double brick mold for making bricks by hand. This one came from West Virginia and is in the author's collection.

EXCERPTS FROM ACCOUNT BOOK OF ITHAMAR SPAULDING

1795

April 24 we all worked at Jones underpining till brakefaft & then we all went to Bonds chimney

25 we all worked at Bonds chimneys & Hunt went of in the afternoon Shattuck & Joseph went to J. Jones to stay over Sunday

May 16 my self & Joseph mended Mr. Hunftables fireplaces.

June 1 I worked at Mr. Nathan Barett pulling down & building chimneys & Joseph came from Pepperell

July 2 my Self & Joseph Spauldin worked for Peter Wheeler all day building Shop Chimneys

29 I worked 1 or 2 hours in the forenoon & all the afternoon for Jofhua Lawrance building his Shop chimneys & Joseph worked for J. Jones & they finifhed his brick houfe

30 we both worked at Jofhua Lawrances Shop Chimneys $\frac{1}{2}$ the forenoon & in the afternoon it rained & we did but a little

August 4 Joseph worked in ye Shop in ye forenoon & I worked in ye forenoon at Jofh. Lawrances Shop chimneys $\frac{1}{3}$ of a day, in ye afternoon at Afa Heywoods making plaftering morter both off us

31 both at Minott chimneye, only I was at home $1\frac{1}{2}$ hour with Mr. Wiman from Woburn

Sept 5 both at Sten. Minott chimneys

15 I was in ye Shop making J. Jones chimneys pieces

25 I was doing but little & set J. Jones chimney pieces & Joseph worked for Asa Heywood in ye afternoon laying ye hatchway & door step

26 I worked in all ye day one $\frac{1}{2}$ of it for J. Jones laying a hearth & plaftering & Joseph was in ye shop

28 Joseph & my self went to work for Mr. Jonathan Butterick puling down & building chimneys in ye morning.

Oct 8 Both at Jonathan Buttericks till Brakefast & then we finifhed his chimneys & came home & did a little in ye shop the work we did for J. Butterick came to 14 dollars.

14 both in ye shop only I mended Patty Heartshorn chimney & received my pay of her.

Oct 22 I worked for Mr Ned. Flint building chimneys all day & Joseph worked for Joseph I. Emerfon at Mr. Jno. Richardfons

23 I was at Ned. Flints in ye fore noon & in ye afternoon it rained, & Joseph worked for Mr. Emerfon at Richardfons—shop from 9 o clock to 12.—& in ye afternoon we layed a stone hearth for Wam. Heywood

24 I worked for Ned. Flint all day & finifhed his chimneys & Joseph was in ye shop

30

29   I white-wafhed a little for Dea. White & pointed round Mr. Merricks Chimneys & Joseph in ye shop

30   I was building a fireplace for Abijah Flint all day & Joseph in ye shop

Nov 9   I worked for Mr. Joseph Mulikin building chimneys all day & Joseph was at home in ye forenoon in ye afternoon at Mr. Mulikins

11   both at Mr. Noah Morfes building chimneys all day, only Joseph stayed at home till brakefaft

17   we worked for Mr. Mulikin all day & in the evening laid a hearth for Mr. Morfe

23   Joseph in ye Shop & turned a trimmed & laid a herth for Mr. J. Muliken 2/
26   We both flaftered for Mr. Wright at Mulikens Shop for which I am to have 8/
& I laid the herth for Mulliken & turned the arch under it 2/6
& Joseph finifhed Mr. Morfes pointing & herth 1/6

30   both in ye shop only I pointed—chimneys

Dec. 3   both in ye shop only I worked for John Merick Esq.

4   I worked for John Merrick Esq. till 2 or 3 o clock & finifhed his stove & herth and Joseph worked at Mr. Brifter Freemans in ye afternoon

5   I worked at Dea. Whites all day setting a stove & boarded myself 7/6 & found 112 bricks which I had of Mr. Ami White 3/0 and Joseph worked for Abner Wheeler at a school house at Lincoln until the sun one hour high at night

12   both in ye shop only we worked on the top of Mr. Muliken chimney some 2/6

17   we laid 2 herths for Mr. Dix & found 140 bricks the work for the hearths 6/

Stove Back from the Webster Furnace located in Lancaster County, Pennsylvania, 1748
Courtesy Pennsylvania Farm Museum of Landis Valley.

5

THE IRON WORKS

It has no doubt been very noticeable that the objects in and around the fireplaces illustrated in this volume were made predominantly of iron. In pioneer days this was necessary for utensils used over a fire. Just as bricks played a most important part in chimney building, so did iron play a major role in providing a supply of tools and utensils for the fireplace.

The first successful ironworks in America was established about 1646 in Saugus, Massachusetts. In the years of its operation, until 1670, the Saugus Ironworks manufactured iron and iron products which were vitally needed by our Colonial forebears. There were other ironworks throughout the Colonies, to be sure, especially in Rhode Island, Connecticut, New Jersey, Maryland, Delaware, North Carolina and Pennsylvania. Pennsylvania had a good supply of all the materials needed: limestone, iron ore and charcoal. An iron furnace seemed to spring up wherever iron ore or bog iron was found in sufficient quantity, where limestone could be obtained, and where water power was available nearby. The charcoal was man made.

The furnaces required an enormous amount of charcoal which was produced by means of the charcoal pits. Trees were cut from nearby forests and reduced to about four foot lengths of wood. These logs were stacked in a pyramidal shape with an open space at the bottom for firing. The stacked logs were then covered over with clay or sod to exclude the air, except for a control opening at the base and an opening at the top for draught. After lighting the wood, it was left to smudge and char for a few days. During this time the pit was tended to keep it stirred up, if necessary, or to limit the supply of air in order to keep the fire from breaking out, which would destroy the wood which was to become charcoal.

Charcoal generates a hotter fire than coal. For this reason it was ideal for iron furnaces and the blacksmith's forge. It proved desirable

A replica of the first cast iron pot made in America at the Saugus Iron Works.

also for use in the small household braziers since it burns with neither smoke nor flame.

Ironworks is a broad term which covers several distinct operations in the manufacture of iron. Charcoal was usually made on the grounds of the ironworks as it had to be abundant and readily available. The blast furnace constituted the second operation in making iron, as the charcoal pit was the first. The furnace had an opening in the top through which the iron ore, the limestone, and charcoal were poured and burned together. This process eliminated impurities and fluxed the iron. The molten metal thus produced was run out of the furnace through a hole in the bottom, and into sand molds to form bars of iron called pig iron or into special molds to form cast iron utensils. These utensils were durable and heavy but could break, whereas wrought iron was flexible and could be welded or shaped by a blacksmith.

Another feature or part of the ironworks was the forge, which housed the fineries and chafery where cast iron bars were converted into wrought iron by reheating and pounding with a huge hammer. The wrought iron, how-

ever, was not ready for the blacksmith or other ironworker until the bars had been reheated still again and rolled into "flats." Some of the "flats" were slit into rods which were used chiefly in making nails. These last two operations were accomplished by a rolling and slitting mill.

Here then we have the source of iron in America as exemplified by the Saugus Restoration, which recently has been designated as a National Historic Landmark. The Saugus Ironworks is supposed to have turned out the first cast iron pot, a one quart size, to be made in this country. There is a record also that one or more remaining firebacks were made at Saugus. The part the blacksmith played in producing fireplace utensils is described in a separate chapter.

This chapter has presented only a brief sketch of the ironworks which contributed so essentially to homes and farms of the Colonists, and in particular, the fireplaces of Early America. Those who wish to delve deeper into the technical aspects of the Ironworks can find adequate treatment in other volumes, some of which are listed in the bibliography.

33

A fireback cast in an early American foundry, which is in one of the six fireplaces in the home of the author.

Fireframe in parlor of Fitch House, Old Sturbridge Village.

6

THE BLACKSMITH

Inasmuch as Longfellow has a secure place in this book, I will quote the well-known poem on the village smithy.

> Under a spreading chestnut tree
>   The village smithy stands;
> The smith, a mighty man is he,
>   With large and sinewy hands;
> And the muscles of his brawny arms
>   Are strong as iron bands.

The author has had experience with blacksmiths, having had horses shod when a young man and more recently having fireplace andirons, implements and tools repaired or made. The last job a smithy did for the author was one of the smithy's last also, but he worked at his trade until he was ninety-three years old —a remarkable man, who had started in as a young man shoeing horses for the army.

The author has recently dismantled the shop, having purchased all the tools and equipment. This transaction was coincidental and had no connection with the subject matter of this chapter except that it impressed me with the dust and grime which accumulates over the years in a blackened, dark smithy shop.

One has only to read a blacksmith's ledger to know how important this artisan was to the community. From reading two pages of a Hopkinton, New Hampshire, blacksmith's ledger it can be seen that fireplace tools and utensils as well as farm and home hardware were newly made or repaired at the smithy's shop. The major part of his work, however, was shoeing horses and oxen and making nails.

One of the principal products of the rolling and slitting mills at the iron works was rods from which nails were made. Before the rods were produced in this country, they were imported from Europe. Nails were in great demand because of the new buildings required to house and serve the colonists. That nails and spikes were scarce at first is evidenced by the use of wooden pegs in the construction of barns and much furniture.

Courtesy of Shelburne Museum, Shelburne, Vermont

BLACKSMITH AND WHEELWRIGHT SHOP

Shelburne Museum, Shelburne, Vermont

The shop is old, an original one, which was moved from Shelburne Village to its present location in 1956. The earliest reference to the shop to be found is dated 1840. John Dubuc, a Canadian, was the first known blacksmith to occupy the shop. It is a brick structure and contains the forge, tools, and shoeing frame.

Sam Hanna, who has made documentary films of Old English Crafts says, "The interior of a blacksmith's forge was always dim, and the reason for this was it enabled him to see the colour of the hot iron from which he estimated the working temperature of the iron."

Farmers became nail making blacksmiths in many instances. The kitchen fireside often was the scene of nail making. With anvil, tools and nail rods the farmer blacksmith used the fireplace as a forge to heat the end of a rod white hot. Then it was cut into short lengths and shaped before the iron cooled. Nail making by individual farmers did not infringe too much on the local blacksmith, who had as much or more than he could do.

Blacksmiths came to the new country as did bricklayers, with the first ships. Fortunately for their work and for the colonists, iron ore and bog iron was found in sufficient supply to serve foundries which sprang up along the seaboard and near the early settlements. The iron which was cast by the foundries was molded into utensils and hardware, but much of it was turned into wrought iron and supplied to blacksmiths for their use in the form of rods.

The blacksmith turned out much of the fireplace equipment, in fact all of it, except for the cast iron pots and kettles. The tools of the fireplace were fashioned by the blacksmith to include the crane, pot hooks, eyes to fasten the crane, andirons, trammels, shovels, pokers and tongs. The utensils include in part, the oven peels, griddles, toasters, trivets, ladles, skewers and skewer holders, forks, spatulas, pans and kettles. Is there any wonder that the now disappearing blacksmith was indispensable to every colonial community?

The fireplace was just one area; the whole household and the farm required his services. A glance through the pages of the ledger will tell the story of how he mended the kettle, the rim of a wheel, the runner of a sleigh and hundreds of other repair jobs which kept the early settlers "in business." For years there were no stores—a new article had to be made or an old article had to be repaired.

A reference in the autobiography of Lyman Beecher W.W. is apropos. He wrote,

> Nathaniel Beecher, the son of Joseph, was my grandfather. He was not quite so strong as his father, being only able to lift a barrel of cider into a cart. He was six feet tall and a blacksmith by trade. His anvil stood on the stump of the old oak tree under which Davenport preached the first sermon. Just the place for a strong man to strike while the iron was hot and hit the nail on the head.

Courtesy of Shelburne Museum
Shelburne, Vermont

THE FOREST AND WOOD FIRES

The author quotes from the *History of Warner* by Harriman in the chapter on the potash. Harriman wrote:

In those days families burnt vast amounts of fuel, their fireplaces being large and open and their houses being unfinished and cold. They cared not how much they burnt. Firewood was abundant and cheap.

So it was. The forest was everywhere, so to speak, and clearings had to be made before agriculture could exist. Trees were felled not only to get them out of the way but to provide wood for the fireplace and wood for lumber, the important building material. Houses, barns, furniture, wagons, sleighs and ships were made almost entirely of wood in the days of our forefathers. However, no product is inexhaustible, and this was evident when iron works were established. Charcoal was needed for the furnaces, and to make charcoal, quantities of wood were required.

In terms of wood for the fireplace, the forest was vital. For example, when a minister

was settled by a community, he would be paid so much in cash plus his wood supply. Harriet Beecher Stowe tells about a "wood spell" in *Old Town Folks*. The wood spell was a day set aside when every parishioner would bring a sled load of wood to the minister's home.

Every family, not only the minister, had to have a mighty pile of wood. All the men contributed to the joint effort. Wood was needed in the warm months for cooking and for warmth as well in the cold months. In one of her books, which she autographed for the author, Marion Nicholl Rawson wrote "He who cuts his own wood is twice warmed." She may have been quoting Henry Thoreau.

There is more to burning wood successfully and efficiently, than meets the eye. A fire in a fireplace should have balance. There should be a large back log of slow burning wood against which the fire is burned and which contributes to the blaze. Also there should be a lesser front log, and in between still smaller wood. In renewing the fire, wood should be placed at the back of the fire and not in front where the burning brands should be.

In order to obtain more flame for light, finely split resinous or pitch pine wood was thrown on top of the fire. A good deal of the family's home work was done by the flaring light of such splinters or knots of pine called candlewood in the North and lightwood in the South. Captain John Smith wrote in 1628,

> They have wood enough if they will cut it over, at their doors to make fires, and candels could be made from the oyle in the splinters of the fir trees.

An Englishman by the name of W. Robinson was so enamored of wood fires that he wrote a book extolling the virtues of wood. He converted a number of fireplaces back to wood burning in a large house to be purchased. He said that,

> The secret of fireplace management is a plentiful supply of ashes kept at the level of the andirons

He further stated that,

> It is not generally realized that a wood fire can be kept burning night and day in a fireplace with very little attention and with a small consumption of wood.

We do know that a well banked fire will keep from eight to twelve hours and will send some heat from the hot bricks all of this time.

By turning the ashes over in the morning embers will be found sufficient to start the fire for the day, especially with the aid of a small faggot or bellows.

If one has a good fireplace screen or a wide hearth, half burned brands may be pulled off the fire at bedtime. These brands should be stood on one side of the fireplace, and they will soon burn out, but will be of use in making the fire the next morning. This has been a practice of the author. A well banked fire at night also reduces the danger of fire. In England during the reign of William the Conqueror, the bells were rung by law at seven in the evening so that all might cover the fire and extinguish the lights.

It was in England that the curfew was invented, a perforated cover of sheet brass, with a handle, which was placed over the remaining embers after they were collected in the chimney recess. The curfew was a safety measure which at the same time preserved some embers until the next morning. The old metal curfew is very rare, and the author has never seen one in America. But the word curfew remains, with the meaning that when a bell or whistle announces a certain time in the evening, all young people should be at home and in bed. When the author was a boy in Missouri, the "curfew" rang at nine p.m. and it was heeded.

THE POTASH

The town of Warner, New Hampshire, has been the vacation and weekend home for the author and his family for some forty years. With the old farm house, which we purchased in 1935, came a *History of Warner from 1735 to 1879* by Walter Harriman. In the pages of this volume, the "Potash" was referred to quite vividly. What Mr. Harriman called a potash, the term used in the town records, Marion Nicholl Rawson, an author and antiquarian, referred to as an "Ashery."

According to the records, the proprietors of Amesbury in March 1766, voted that three men should have eighty acres of land provided they set up a potash. Mr. Harriman reported that the potash was built on "a very small plot of ground" and that "the sills were much lower than the road and the ashes were carried in over the beams on an inclined bridge."

Every ten bushels of ashes, according to the practice then followed, entitled a man to a gill of West India rum as a gratuity. This was in addition to the going price of his commodity. In those days, says Harriman, "families burnt vast amounts of fuel, their fireplaces being large and open . . . firewood was abundant and cheap, and while there was not 'millions in it,' there was ashes in it, and there was rum in the ashes." Harriman explained that the early settlers of Warner were about an average class, and they had their appetites and weaknesses in common with the race.

All of the above only goes to show that ashes were an important by-product of the fireplace. The Potash or Ashery was simply a place for keeping and rendering the ashes which were surplus to the individual family needs. They were a salable commodity. Besides being used for potash as fertilizer, the ashes were used to provide lye in soap making, and for hulling corn and in making saleratus or pearlash. The potashes (repositories) were quite numerous in the Colonies, for the settlers in this country were making all of their own potash until about 1850.

The brick ovens, as well as the fireplace,

were a source of ashes, and a space beneath the oven was usually provided in which to store the ashes from the oven. Hard wood was used chiefly in the ovens and this made the best ash.

In the Wendell Davis house in Hampton Connecticut, there is a very unusual ash storage space in the cellar. An opening in the stone work of the back wall of the fireplace is just large enough for a shovel, to dump ashes directly below into a beehive storage "well" which is built into the chimney foundation. The cellar opening into this "well" is not much larger than the one in the fireplace, but it permits the winter's supply of ashes to be removed when needed.

Potashes had leaching vessels such as a barrel or a hollowed section of a tree trunk. A leaching stone or board would be placed underneath the vessel, and these had a trough to catch the liquor as it ran off. There is a leaching stone at Old Sturbridge Village, and a leaching board of the author's is illustrated.

Individual families got their lye for making soap and other uses, by the same process. For example, in a barrel alternate layers of ashes and straw would be placed and hot water would be poured in the top of the barrel. As the water seeped through it became a potash liquid which would flow down the trough into a receptacle. This process was called leaching.

A lye board for use in draining the lye. It is placed under the barrel of ashes and straw through which hot water is poured. Few lye boards have survived.

The liquid which was drawn off was put in an iron kettle for boiling over the fire, until it became a dark thickish residue of potash and when still further reduced and purified by baking it became pearlash—a baking powder. In many potashes the leaching, boiling for potash and the baking for pearlash was done, one process after the other.

The first step in making soap was the same as in making potash. The ashes were leached and the lye was procured in this way. From this point on the process differs. It was necessary that the lye be exactly strong enough and when at the right strength * it was put in a

* The lye could be made to gather strength by repeated pourings over still more ashes until it would float an egg. It took about six bushels of ashes with four times as many pounds of grease to make a barrel of soap.

copper or brass kettle or pot which already had in it the soap fat, from cookings or killings, in proper amount. The lye was poured in slowly and stirred continuously in one direction while the mixture boiled. At the right time the product—a dark colored mass—was poured into a tub which might have been kept in the cellar. The soap thus made was jelly-like in softness and was used by "spoonfuls" rather than cakes. However, hard soap could be made of very sour cream mixed with lye.

So it was that the alkali of common wood ashes was needed for soap making, to hull corn for hominy, for potash and for pearlash. The Early American Fireplace played an important part in providing these products.

Two large cast iron kettles which could well have been used in soap making.

9

CANDLEMAKING AND ILLUMINATION OF THE PIONEER HOME

CANDLEMAKING

The making of candles was a "before the fireplace" operation for either the dipping or molding process. An outside fire could be used, but generally the work was done at the big fireplace, where hot water and melted tallow could be readily available.

Candlemaking was done in cool weather so that the tallow would harden after dipping, or after being poured into a mold. Tallow or suet that had been saved was cut up and boiled in a big iron pot for refining. While melting, the tallow was stirred from time to time. After it liquefied, it was strained.

Candlemaking was essentially a craft or home industry, but there were a number of itinerant candlemakers who, like the cobblers and pewterers, made periodic visits through the countryside to help with candlemaking, especially after the advent of molds, which the itinerant could bring with him. It was not long, however, before every household had one or more molds.

The two principal methods of candlemaking were dipping and molding. Some beeswax candles were made by "forming", or rolling the wax around a wick, but this method was relatively unimportant. Bayberry candles were dipped, and tallow candles were made by both dipping and molding.

Dipping was an earlier method of candlemaking, but there is no clear date when molds and the molding process were introduced. By dipping was meant the practice of dipping the wick into melted tallow until enough wax had adhered to form a candle. This sounds simple enough, but to make tallow dips successfully a number of steps had to be followed and followed correctly:

In the first place, the wicking had to be prepared by cutting a number of pieces to even lengths, generally about nine inches long. Often the length of the wick was determined by the depth of the kettle which held the tallow.

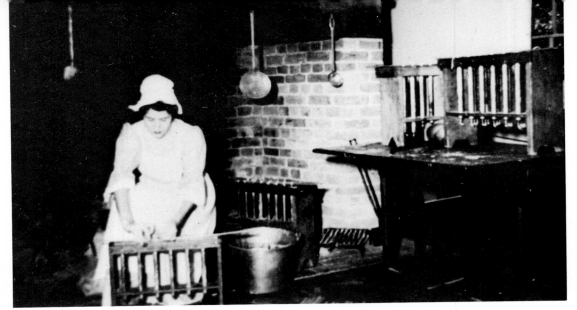
Using pewter molds in front of the fireplace.

Next, a number of "candle rods" about eighteen inches long and about a quarter of an inch in diameter were needed. The length of the rods was determined by the diameter of the kettle and the number of wicks to be put in it. The strands were placed about two and a half inches apart so that all of them could go into the kettle at the same time but without interfering with each other. Each length of wicking was looped over a rod and twisted. By dipping the fingers of one hand into the melted tallow when not too hot, and coating the twisted wicks, the loose ends would stay together and, as the tallow hardened, the wicks became straight and firm.

While this preparation was going on, a large kettle of water would be heating over the fire into which the strained tallow was poured to a depth of two or three inches more than a long candle's length. The tallow rose to the surface of the water, forming a layer on top. Then the wicks were dipped into the tallow. The first dip was in wax only, the level of which was kept constant by adding either tallow or hot water as necessary.

Note: It was claimed that soaking the wick in borax or salt would keep the string from burning down too rapidly when the finished candles were in use.

After each dipping the rods were placed across two poles set between two chairs. When the tallow had hardened enough it was dipped again and again until the desired circumference had been obtained. The tallow in the kettle could be reheated if it started to harden, and any roughness on the candle could be removed by scraping with a knife.

The process of dipping ended by hanging the dips on a hook or a "dryer," and finally, after the candles had properly hardened, they were put in a wooden box awaiting their turn to be placed near the fire in a "candle box," usually made of tin.

Making candles in molds succeeded the practice of dipping and was generally preferred after the molds became available. The molds were usually made of tin, but a few were of pewter, and still fewer of ceramics or pottery. The pewter and pottery tubes were contained in a wooden frame, whereas the tin tubes were held together by a flat tin top and bottom. With few exceptions, each cluster of tin tubes had one or two handles at the top. Mr. L. M. A. Roy, in his pictorial book on candlemaking says that a cluster making one dozen candles was most widely used. The author has a single tube mold, a two, three, four, six and so on to a forty-eight,

CANDLE MOLDS

Tin molds of one, two, three, four and twenty-four tubes.

A twelve candle mold made of pewter in a wooden frame and a tin frame which contains one hundred forty-four tubes.

Candle boxes for "storing" candles.

and then a 144 cluster which was a veritable factory.

Wicks also were essential to molding, and they were generally made of loosely spun cotton which had to be cut long enough to go through the mold with enough to spare at each end for tying. From four to six strands made up each wick. There was no need to grease or oil the mold, but it had to be clean and dry. A piece of thin wire with a hook at one end could be used to draw the wick through the tubes. At the bottom end of the molds, which is the small end of the tubes, knots were tied in the wicks to keep the ends in place, although no knots were needed if a double length wick was used and drawn down one tube and up another.

After the wicks at the bottom end were properly tied or in place, the mold was turned right side up. The wicks on top were put in place by dividing the strands of each wick and tying the two ends around a skewer or small wooden rod. The wicks were then centered in the tubes, and everything was ready for the tallow to be poured into the mold and around the wicks. The mold was then set in a cool place to harden.

When the tallow had hardened, the knots or loops at the bottom were cut and the mold was dipped into a kettle of hot water which softened the tallow in the mold slightly, allowing the candles to be withdrawn. By holding the mold with one hand and pulling the wooden skewers with the other, the candles slid easily from the mold.

The candles which were molded with their tops down were now ready for storage. They needed to be hung in a cool place for four or five days to harden. Like the dipped candles, they finally got to a candle box near the fireplace where they could be lighted with a spill * after the spill had been lighted from the fireplace fire.

* a spill—a slender piece of wood or paper (twisted) for lighting candles, lamps, etc.

45

CANDLEMAKING

The dipping process in use at the Fitch House at Old Sturbridge Village.

The kettle on the table contains hot wax or tallow which was melted over the fire. In this case bayberry wax is being used. The wicks are fastened to a rod or stick for dipping. When the desired size is attained after many dippings, the rods are placed across two poles which are supported by two chairs, for drying. *Courtesy of Old Sturbridge Village.*

Pan lamp, "hog scraper" candlesticks, Betty lamp, from the author's collection.

Rare folding double rush holder and candle sockets on adjustable ratchet.

ILLUMINATION OF THE PIONEER HOME

One of the uses of the fireplace was for candlemaking, and the light from candles supplemented the firelight. Oftentimes resinous wood of pine trees was tossed on the fireplace fire to get a brighter glow. In the South the pitchy wood of the pine tree was called lightwood and farther north it was called candlewood. The resinous pine was abundant along the whole seacoast so the early settlers had the splint or torch, the candle, and the rushlight available to them by their own labors, but few homes had lamps of any kind, and these came from England in the earliest days of our Colonies. The records do show that there were some lighting devices of tin, pewter or brass in this period.

In Salem, Massachusetts, in the year 1935, a Pioneer Village was set up which portrayed the life of the pioneer. Special exhibits were sponsored by groups or firms by reason of their special interest. The exhibit of Artificial Illumination was sponsored by the Hygrade Sylvania Corporation. The description of this exhibit is so well stated that the author asked for and received permission to reproduce it. I am, therefore, using it in its entirety. I have been a collector of early lighting devices and have lectured on the subject many times, and I would not change a word of it. I would, however, add that saucer lamps were often called pan lamps and wick channel lamps were also called cruisies or grease lamps.

The lamps, of which there are small drawings for illustration, were used about the fireplace and in the fireplace room which was the center of home life. Those lighting devices were auxiliaries, so to speak, of the fireplace light, in the homes which could afford them. In the fireplace photographs quite a number of the different lighting devices will be noted, and some are shown among the "utensil" illustrations.

Save-all or "kitchen candlestick"—tinder box from the author's collection.

Rush holders with rush lights from the author's collection.

Right and left: pierced tin lanterns. Center: a lantharn from the author's collection.

ARTIFICIAL ILLUMINATION CHART

TORCHES AND SPLINTS

Pitchy wood from pine trees, used as a torch outdoors, and as a splint, when held by crude iron supports indoors.

CANDLES

Use of candles during pioneer days was limited, due to fact that only wealthy could afford them. They were made from fats of wild animals, from tallow of domestic animals; and sometimes from the bayberry. Candlesticks of the period were made of tin, iron, brass or pewter.

RUSHLIGHTS

Poorer people used rushes for lighting, stripping the bark from the dried stock, and soaking it in fat or grease. Special holders were devised to support the rushlights, and these are known as rushlights or rushlight holders.

LAMPS

In very few homes during pioneer days were lamps a part of the household equipment, though records show that a few made of tin, iron, pewter or brass were in use from the earliest days. Poorer people used a saucer filled with animal fat or fish oil, using a rag laid against the saucer's edge as a wick.

SAUCER LAMPS

Most simple in form was the saucer lamp, in which a shallow bowl served as a reservoir. This was commonly made of iron and had an arm with a hook attached so that it could be hung where desired.

WICK CHANNEL LAMPS

In appearance these lamps resembled a half pear lying on its side, the body being the reservoir and the tapering part the wick channel. Both this type and the saucer lamp were liable to drop oil.

PHOEBE LAMPS

Double wick channel lamps, called Phoebes, were similar in form to the above type in general appearance, but were used in pairs, one above the other. The upper lamp, which was the reservoir, hung from the arm of the lower lamp, which served as the drip bowl. Overflow was collected in this way, thus conserving fuel. The two sections could also be used separately.

BETTY LAMPS

The covered wick channel lamp, now called the Betty Lamp, was in use only in the wealthier homes. A support for the wick was incorporated in the nose of the lamp, keeping the wick back from the edge to prevent overflow. The reservoir was covered, and a movable lid provided for filling and cleaning. A wick pick always accompanied these lamps, in the form of a piece of wire attached to the arm by a chain.

TINDER BOXES AND LANTHORNES

Other appliances in use were candle boxes for the storage of candles, extinguishers and snuffers, and savealls which permitted the candles to be entirely consumed. Tinder boxes, for striking fire, were to be found in many homes, and lanterns, then called lanthornes because thin pieces of horn were used in place of the glass in later lanterns, served the pioneer both indoors and out.

Sponsored by Hygrade Sylvania Corporation   *Courtesy of Pioneer Village, Salem, Mass.*

10

DYEING AND THE INDIGO DYEPOT

The Colonists liked color for their clothing, except for the Quakers who wore only grey and white. Dyeing was an important part of early American life. Materials used as the source of dyes included hickory bark, sassafras bark, madder, maple bark, sumac, indigo, red oak bark, butternut bark, cochineal and saffron.

A chart of wool samples dyed with old time dyes by Mrs. Etheljane Schetky, hangs on the wall of historic Cocumscussoc or Smith's Castle, in Wickford, Rhode Island. Three shades are shown in which indigo is the sole or participating dye: black walnut and indigo, indigo, and oak bark and indigo.

The old earthenware dyepot was made in a number of different sizes, and was so called regardless of size. It was unglazed on the outside and usually glazed on the inside. Some had covers and some did not. The indigo dyepot was the only one which had a connection with the fireplace.

Indigo was not raised north of South Carolina, and the manufacture of the dye was limited largely to the southern area where it was a profitable business for many years. The more northerly Colonists obtained their indigo at first from peddlers who made their rounds once or twice a year. Later, shops carried indigo and other dyes.

The *Boston Newsletter* of March 17, 1712 carried an advertisement which read,

> To be sold by Zabdiel Boylston, at his apothecary shop in Dock Square, Boston, viz. the finest Spanish powder, blew starch and indigo, painters colors, alum copperas.

In simple terms the process of indigo manufacture was to take a part of the leaf of the plant and, by fermentation, turn it into a violet blue substance. To perform this process, a vat for rotting the plant was needed, another vat for beating it, and a place for drying the end result. Indigo was a familiar household word in the early days. A place was reserved for the indigo dyepot at one side of the open hearth, a pot which would generally hold at least two gallons.

A cover was almost essential, as a principal

Cupboard in weaving room at Old Sturbridge Village in which is kept an exhibit of sample materials from which dyes of different colors are obtained.

Exhibit of yarn dyed with natural dyes by Mrs. Lawrence Schetky. Now at Cocumscussoc or Smith's Castle, North Kingston, Rhode Island.

On each end is an earthenware dye pot. Their color is brown. They are glazed inside and rough outside. In the center is a wooden churn. The indigo dye pot was kept on the hearth.

51

ingredient of the prepared indigo was carefully saved urine. The dyepot was never allowed to be an odor nuisance, however, for in addition to the cover there was always a bag of ashes or root of sweet flag floating in the mixture to quench any odor. The dyepot was even used as a seat by children on occasion. It was kept close to the fire because the dye had to be kept warm always.

So it was that indigo was tied up with the home center by occupying a respectable place on the hearth. The indigo had its place for many years in turning the drab and the plain into colorful and bright garments, bed quilts, and other home furnishings. While the indigo dyepot was kept on the hearth, the fireplace was also the scene of operation in home dyeing with natural colors.

Generally, two processes were involved, mordanting and dyeing. Mordanting refers to the application of a substance for the purpose of fixing the color upon the fiber to be dyed. This substance had to be capable of fusing with the coloring matter which was used. Many early mordants were household staples such as salt, vinegar, soda, cream of tartar, or lye. Also used were the metallic salts of alum, iron and tin.

In mordanting or dyeing, the fireplace was a necessary facility, along with a copper kettle for heating the water used in the process. In preparing the dye bath the plant material was boiled. The dye bath itself, however, with the fiber to be dyed in it, was simmered, never boiled. The early American housewife learned the proper temperatures by experience, just as she did in the case of heating water and tallow for candlemaking.

46   THE COUNTRY DYER's

till the colour is obtained. After this rinfe and dry it for dreffing.

N. B. If there be two drafts, or packs of cloth to colour; take out part of the liquor, that the dye may equally colour each pack, by occafionally adding the liquor again as you need it.

CHAP VIII.

For Saxon Blue.

BY one fimple procefs, this colour is obtained. All the utenfils nuft be perfectly clean; the water in the copper be brought to boil.

Then put in a fmall quantity of the compound made of oil of vitriol and Indigo; after this let it boil for a few minutes; the cloth being well wet with warm water, is then to be dipped for half an hour; then take it up to cool. Follow this procefs of dipping

ASSISTANT.   47

and cooling until you obtain the colour you defire.

N. B. The reel muft be turned brifkly and the cloth kept open as it runs.

CHAP. IX.

For Snuff Brown.

TAKE twenty yards of fulled cloth, run it in a Copperas liquor, the fame as for Navy blue. Rinfe the cloth, empty the copper. Next fill it with clean water, put in ten pounds of Fuftick chips and one bufhel of Butternut bark; boil them for four or five hours; then dip the cloth for half an hour; take it up to cool, and follow the procefs of dipping and cooling, till you obtain the colour defigned.

Hemlock bark will anfwer, as a fubftitute, for Butternut; but its colour is not fo good, nor fo durable.

A facsimile of a page from *The Country Dyer's Assistant* by Asa Ellis, Jun., published in 1798 in Brookfield, Massachusetts. This old volume on dyeing is owned by the author's wife.

11

PEWTER CASTING

Just as indigo dye, among many dyes, had a fireplace connection, so does the molding of pewter spoons especially relate to the fireplace. In addition, authorities on the making of pewter articles refer to bullet making from pewter which must have taken place at the fireside. It is quite probable that pewter buttons and a few other small objects which could be cast in one piece were molded in the home.

Pewter consists mostly of tin, which is alloyed with copper, antimony, and lead in varying proportions, according to the pewterer and the quality desired. Pewter can be spun, wrought or molded. It is the molding process which concerns us here. Some spoon molds are made of iron and occasionally of wood. The best molds for spoons, however, were made of bronze and they were expensive.

There is ample evidence that one mold served a number of homes. There were also itinerant pewterers, and if the reader has already read the chapter on candlemaking it has been observed that the itinerants often supplied the molds and helped with the candlemaking in the homes which could not afford to own molds. The itinerant pewterer took to the road on foot, horseback or buggy, visiting the farms and villagers much as the peddlers did in the early days of America. He carried his tools and an assortment of molds with him, and in so doing he filled a real need.

Spoons were a much used item in the Colonial homes, for cooking and eating. Many of them were made of pewter. The spoons especially needed to be replenished or repaired from time to time, so the traveling pewterer found plenty to do. He could melt down pewter dishes which were worn out and recast them into new pewter spoons. The fireplace was the source of heat for this operation.

The author has so far found no reference to pewter button making in the home, but he does have old pewter buttons in his collections. These were made in molds which might well have been a fireside operation. Button molds probably were passed from house to house as were spoon molds. The Deerfield Memorial Hall has in its collection a spoon mold once owned by one of the first settlers of Greenfield, Mass. It was in this mold that all of his spoons and those of his neighbors were cast.

It seems that bullets too on many occasions were made from pewter in which there was more or less lead content. There is practically no pewter remaining which can be attributed to the 17th Century, which is said to have resulted largely from melting down pewter in order to make pewter bullets during periods of Indian disturbances. During the American Revolution, too, many pewter dishes were turned in by patriotic women for the casting of bullets to help establish American independence. So it is that the early American fireplace played its part in the birth of a new nation.

In the chapter on Candlemaking, reference is made to the pewter candle molds, which usually came in a "set" of twelve. These molds seldom came singly, as did tin ones, so far as is now known. The pewter tubes are usually enclosed in a wooden frame which forms a "stand" for the tubes. A photograph of candle-making with pewter molds, at Old Sturbridge Village, is shown. Here again is a fireplace operation, that of making candle "lights" which supplemented the firelight in many instances.

Two pewter spoons. Underneath the spoon handles are the two parts of a bronze spoon mold.

12

FIREPLACE FARE

Our forefathers ate well even if they did have to use an open fire for all their cooking. All along the Atlantic seaboard there was fish to be had from salt and fresh water. There was ample game in the forests and of great variety. The fields gave forth abundant crops and fruits.

Rev. Francis Higginson, first minister of Massachusetts Bay Colony wrote in 1629,

Excellent vines, also mulberries, plums, rasp-berries, corrance, chestnuts, filberts, walnuts, smalnuts, hurtlberries and of whitethorne neare as good as our cherries in England and they grow plenty here.

Our turnips, parsnips and carrots are here both bigger and sweeter than in England. Pumpions, cowcombers, pot herbs grow abundantly among the grasses. Strawberries, peny-royall, wintersourie, sorrell, brockeline, liver-wort, carwell, watercresses, leeks and onions are ordinaire.

There was, of course, no refrigeration except that provided by nature herself in the winter months, but ways were devised to keep food for a period of time by drying, salting, smoking, pickling or burying in the earth, according to what food was being preserved. The fireplace even played a part by drying certain vegetables and fruits and by smoking hams and other meats.

The Pilgrims procured corn from the Indians until they could raise their own, and it became one of their staple foods. The corn was placed in a large wooden mortar made from a hollow tree trunk, and then pulverized with a wooden pestle. When sifted it was ready for use. Some of it was mixed with water and put in a bake kettle to make johnny-cake. Some was rolled into balls and put in deep fat to make "jack cake," and some was put in a kettle with salt and water and boiled to make hasty pudding.

John W. Halsy, the "Rhode Island Historian," in writing about the Cocumscussoc House fireplace (see illustration) said,

It was no unusual thing to hang upon the spit a quarter of a lamb or a haunch of venison at the same time that turkey, ducks and fowl were being roasted. The fireplaces in which such cooking was done, were enormous.

RECIPE FOR BEATEN BISCUITS GIVEN BY AN OLD-FASHIONED SOUTHERN COOK

Ob cose I gladly gib de rule
I mak dese biscuits by
But rules don no mo mak a cook
Dan summons mak a Saint

Well, bout de greediencies required
Ob cose you know bout dem
How much to put an when
For when you git dat dough
Mixed up all sweet and neat
Dere's where yo genius gwine to show.

To git dem biscuits beat—
For de homefolks I always gives
Four hundred licks
But when I'se specting company in
I gives Five Hundred Sho'.

Courtesy, Kenmore, Fredericksburg, Va.

BRICK OVEN PLUMB CAKE*

1 cup dark brown sugar
⅜ lb. butter or margarine
  (1½ sticks)
4 eggs, beaten
¼ cup molasses
1 lb. seedless raisins
1 lb currants, plumped
½ lb. citron, chopped
1½ tsps. cloves
1½ tsps. cinnamon
1 tsp. mace or nutmeg
2 cups sifted flour
3 tbsps. sherry
3 tbsps. brandy

Cream butter, mix in sugar until light and fluffy, add beaten eggs and molasses. Add raisins, plumped currants, and citron. Sift the flour with the cloves, cinnamon, and mace and stir in. Mix thoroughly, then stir in the sherry and brandy. Prepare three small loaf pans by greasing them and lining with waxed paper or foil. Spread batter in pans. Bake at 300° for 1½ hours.

*Plumb cake was the old term for fruit cake. Raisins were known as plumbs; hence the term.

from "Hot from the Oven" [19]
Courtesy, Old Sturbridge Village, Sturbridge, Mass.

It is the cooking of food in the fireplace rather than availability, which is the chief interest of this chapter. It seems appropriate, therefore, to present some special old fashioned recipes for the fireplace. Some of these recipes which have survived for many generations are still used today.

The very first recipe which is offered is in reality no recipe at all. It is included to remind us that an experienced cook acquires the "know how" to get results without measures or guide lines. For this "recipe" for "Beaten Biscuits" the author is indebted to Kenmore in Fredericksburg from whence the

Lafayette Ginger Bread recipe was received. The Brick Oven Plumb Cake recipe is taken from a booklet, "Hot from the Oven", published by Old Sturbridge Village. The largest portion of the recipes, by far, were collected by Mrs. Anne Crawford Allen Holst, under the heading, "The Swinging Crane and the Bubbling Pot." This group of old recipes was issued by the Rhode Island Historical Society in 1948.

An article in *New Hampshire Profiles* by Beatrice Vaughn, entitled "Cookery Books from a Past Century," gives some interesting cookery instructions and advice which comes from the olden days. These directions follow the list of ingredients for johnny cake:

> The batter should be mixed thin and poured into a bake kettle and hung uncovered over the open fire until the cake bears the fingers, then set down before the fire.

The same cookbook gave this advice about bear meat,

> Hang your kettle away from the hottest blaze when cooking bear meat, else it will be tough

And suggests that

> bear fat is good for your cooking if you have none from your cattle.

LaFayette Ginger Bread

LaFayette Ginger Bread

MARQUIS de LAFAYETTE returned to America after the Revolutionary War in the fall of 1784. After a stay with his beloved friend, George Washington, at Mt. Vernon, one of the Lewis boys accompanied him to Fredericksburg to pay his respects to the General's mother. They found her in her garden in short gown, petticoat and cap, raking leaves. Unaffectedly she greeted him, and together they went into the house where she made him a mint julep which she served with spiced ginger bread. Listening, with pleased attention, to the Frenchman's praises of her son, her only reply was "George was always a good boy."

In bidding her good bye, General LaFayette asked for her blessing. Lifting her hand, she prayed that the favor of God might be with him always. Deeply moved, he bent and kissed her hand. Young Lewis said, "I had to choke to keep from crying." The Marquis, in commenting on the scene afterwards, said, "I have seen the only Roman matron of my day."

This recipe for LaFayette Ginger Bread, as it was ever after called, was found in an old worn cookery book.

Cut up in a pan ½ cup of the very best fresh butter with ½ cup of excellent brown sugar, beat to a cream with a paddle. Add 1 cup of West India molasses and ½ cup of warm milk; 2 tablespoons of powdered ginger and 1 heaping teaspoon of cinnamon, mace and nutmeg powdered and mixed; 1 wine glass of brandy (I use coffee now). Beat 3 eggs till very light and thick; 3 cups of flour and 1 teaspoon of cream of tartar sifted with flour and stirred alternately with the beaten eggs into the batter. Last, mix in the juice and grated rind of 1 large orange. Dissolve 1 teaspoon of soda in a little warm water, and stir in. Beat until very light. A cup full of seeded raisins is an addition. Bake in a loaf, sheet or patty pans, in a moderate oven.

MRS. VIVIAN MINOR FLEMING,
Honorary Regent Washington-Lewis Chapter, D. A. R.
Fredericksburg, Va.

Courtesy, Kenmore, Fredericksburg, Virginia

THE SWINGING CRANE AND THE BUBBLING POT

Recipes of the Rhode Island Colony
collected by
Anne Crawford Allen Holst

MAIN-DISH PUMPKIN PYE

Medium-size pumpkin	left-over mashed potatoes ⎫ optional
1 or 2 eggs	left-over meat scraps ⎭
Dry bread crumbs	Sage
Black pepper	Salt Butter

Select a firm, ripe pumpkin of a size to suit your family needs—a medium to small-size is best. Wash and scrub the pumpkin well, and slice off the top (the stem end) to make a cover. Scoop out the seeds and fibers from the inside, leaving the meat intact.

Prepare a filling for the pumpkin from dry bread crumbs (whole wheat, Vienna, or rye bread are delicious). If you have any left-over mashed potatoes combine these with the bread crumbs. If you have any left-over meat scraps, these also may be added—chicken is delicious! Add one or two beaten eggs to the filling, and flavor to taste with Sage, black pepper and salt.

Pack the filling into the pumpkin, and place a large piece of butter on top. Replace the cover on pumpkin. Set it in a pie pan with about one inch of water on the bottom to prevent burning, and bake in the oven for one to one and one-half hours, depending on the size. If the water boils away, add more during baking. Serve with the cover on, on a platter.

BOILED DINNER

(Note: Even today this is best made in a pot hung on a crane over the open fire in the fireplace. Such cooking has a flavor all its own!)

"First make sure the fire is good and steady, such as will last until dinner is served. As soon as breakfast is well out of the way, hang on a big pot half full of cold water, and put in a piece of corned beef and a chunk of salt pork. About nine, if the water is boiling hard, put in the pudding, being careful that the cloth has been dipped in scalding water, squeezed dry and floured, before the pudding is placed in it. Put in the beets about the same time. At half-past ten put in the cabbage, at eleven carrots and turnips, and at half-past eleven parsnips and potatoes and squash cut in quarters on top. Serve the pudding first, with butter and molasses. Then dish up the dinner, with beef and pork in the middle of the platter, and the vegetables arranged around them in tasty manner."

BAG PUDDING

1 cup corn meal	1 whole egg
$\frac{1}{4}$ cup white flour	$\frac{1}{2}$ cup raisins
1 cup sour milk	1 teaspoon salt
1 teaspoon soda	

Combine all ingredients, and place in pudding cloth. (A salt sack is very handy to use, treating it as described. Also, as modern fashion dictates, the pudding may be served last, instead of first!)

WICKFORD QUOHAUG PIE

1 pint clams or quohaugs, chopped
1 tablespoon flour
2 tablespoons butter
1 cup water
$\frac{1}{8}$ teaspoon pepper
1 recipe biscuit dough

Cook the flour, butter, pepper and water together until thickened. Put the clams in a deep dish, pour over the cooked sauce, and top with the biscuit dough. Bake in a hot oven.

RYE-AN-INJUN BREAD

1 quart Indian meal
1 pint Rye flour
$\frac{1}{2}$ cup molasses
Yeast

Pour on enough boiling water to scald the cornmeal thoroughly. Set it away to cool, and when it becomes milk-warm, add the rye flour and one cupful yeast (1 cake), and a little salt. Steam for 3 hours, and bake for 1 hour.

BOILED HARD CIDER PIE

1 cup boiled hard cider   2 tablespoons melted butter
2 eggs well beaten   2 tablespoons flour
1 cup sugar   Pastry for 1 pie shell
1 cup water

Combine the sugar and the flour. Add the water, cider and the melted butter. When thoroughly mixed, pour in the beaten eggs and stir well. Pour into the unbaked pie shell, and bake one hour at 350' F.

HUCKLEBERRY JONNY-CAKE

1 cup of R. I. cornmeal
1 heaping cup of huckleberries, more if desired
1 teaspoon sugar
$\frac{1}{3}$ teaspoon salt
Milk
Boiling water

Add sugar and salt to cornmeal, thoroughly scald with boiling water, thin down with milk until medium thin. Add huckleberries. Have griddle hot, and well greased, and fry in small flat cakes. Serves four people.

SWITCHEL

For one gallon, fill the jug with ice, and pour onto the ice in the jug one cupful of molasses, add 2 lemons squeezed and the rind, (or if you have not the lemons, use vinegar) one tablespoonful of ginger, and fill the jug with water.

(Note: Switchel is the drink that seems to be most commonly associated in Rhode Island with haying time. Webster's dictionary says of Switchel: "A drink made with molasses and water sometimes with vinegar, ginger or rum added." Switchel jugs hang in most every old barn hereabouts. A very pleasant drink for hot weather—

ELECTION CAKE

Rub 2 pounds of butter into 5 pints of flour, break together 8 eggs, beat them a little, but do not make them light. Now work these into the butter and flour. Add one cupful of yeast (1 cake), one pint of wine, and knead the whole into a stiff biscuit. Cover, and put aside over night. Next morning add half a pint of seeded raisins, which have been soaked in a gill of brandy over night, also a gill of rose water, 2½ pounds of sugar and one ounce of mace. Work thoroughly and put into a greased loaf cake pan, stand aside again until very light, and bake in a moderate oven about three-quarter of an hour.

CONNECTICUT BEAN PORRIDGE

(Note: There is a saying in Connecticut that "Rhode Islanders make enough Jonny-cakes to stone a well, and Connecticut people make bean porridge enough to fill it!" This recipe was very popular in western Rhode Island.)

"Boil 4 or 5 pounds of corned beef, and save the water in which it was boiled. Take out the beef, and serve. When it is desired to make the bean porridge, add 3 cups of beans which have been soaked, to the corned beef liquid, and cook until the beans are soft. Then add 2 quarts rich new milk. Season to taste with pepper. A simple, hearty dish with plenty of flavor."

HOREHOUND CANDY DROPS

Make a tea (exactly as you would make any other tea) from one-third cup of the horehound herb (dried) and six cups of boiling water, poured on it. To two cups of the tea, add three cups of sugar, and one teaspoon of cream of tartar. Put on stove and boil moderately fast, until the mixture reaches 220 degrees. And one teaspoon butter, but do not stir. Continue cooking mixture to 312 degrees, then take from the fire and add one teaspoon fresh lemon juice, and pour out into shallow buttered pans. As it cools, mark the candy into little squares with a sharp knife, deepening the marking as it grows colder. It can then be easily broken into little squares when the candy is quite cold. Dust these squares with powdered sugar, and pack into clean, dry jars. Yield: about 3 eight-ounce jars of candy.

(Note: Horehound candy is an old New England standby for winter coughs and colds. Those delicious horehound drops are the best cough drops we know of!)

INJUN PUDDING

3 big mixing spoons Indian meal, coarsely ground
2 big mixing spoons Indian meal, finely ground
¾ cup of molasses
grated nutmeg
3 quarts milk
2 tablespoons butter

Take an earthenware beanpot, and grease the inside well with butter. Put into it the five large mixing spoons of Indian meal. Add salt to taste. For a 4 quart beanpot, you should use 3 quarts of milk. Take one quart of the milk, and bring it to a boil. When boiling rapidly, pour over the meal, and stir well to remove all lumps. Add the molasses, stirring well, and the grated nutmeg to taste. Now, very gently, pour on the 2 quarts of COLD milk. Do not stir, simply pour the milk on top without stirring. Cut the butter into bits, and place on top of the pudding, around the edge. Put it into the oven immediately, and bake three hours. DO NOT STIR AT ALL AFTER ADDING THE

COLD MILK, OR WHILE BAKING. If it browns too quickly, cover the pot. Serve with whipped cream or ice cream, for a modern touch! Delicious!

BARBERRIES IN BUNCHES

1 pint syrup   Barberries

First prepare some small pieces of clean white wood, about three inches long, and a quarter-inch wide. Then tie the fruit to the sticks in nice bunches. Have ready a clear sugar syrup (the amount depending on the number of bunches of barberries you wish to preserve). Place the barberry bunches in the syrup, and simmer them in it for half an hour on two successive days. Cover them each time with the syrup when cold. When the fruit looks perfectly clear, they are sufficiently done, and should be stored away in small pots with the sugar syrup poured over.

BARBERRY JELLY

Wash your barberries in cold water, allowing much of the water to remain on them. Place equal quantities of loaf sugar and the wet, ripe barberries in a jar with a close-fitting lid. Place the jar in a tin half-full of boiling water, and set on the stove, or in a moderate oven, and simmer gently for 2 hours.

Strain the juice into a preserving pan, and to each pound of juice, add one pound of sugar. Boil for about 10 minutes, skimming the scum off as it rises. Pour into small pots and seal. A most delicious jelly.

(Note: Barberry Jelly—a big spoonful in a glass of cold water was given to feverish patients to drink, in days gone by. Old Doctor Eldredge of East Greenwich, always recommended this cooling and soothing drink for feverish patients. And how children love it!)

HASTY PUDDING, or How to Make Mush

Put a lump of butter the size of an egg into a quart of boiling water, make it sufficiently thick with corn meal and a little salt, mix perfectly smooth and stir till it is thoroughly done. Serve for supper with rich new milk, or molasses for the children.

(Note: This is what the young Brown children were served for supper, when their nurse would come to the side door of James Brown's house and call, in a voice that could be clearly heard down to Market Square: 'Nicky! Joesy! Johnny! Mosey! Come and get your Mush and 'Lasses!")

HULLED CORN

4 quarts dried white corn   3 cups pure wood ashes

Be sure and use Rhode Island Flint Corn if you can get it. Cook corn in boiling water until nearly tender, then add 3 cups wood ashes to the boiling corn. Let boil until the corn turns a pinkish red, then drain and wash thoroughly in cold running water, until the black center "eyes" of the corn are all out. Begin boiling again in fresh water, then drain, to remove all taste of ashes should any remain. Cook corn until tender, if serving at once. But if for future use, simply dry and store. Makes a wonderful breakfast cereal, served with sugar and milk, or it may be served with butter as a vegetable. Samp—that standby of New England meals—was made of pounded or ground hulled corn, and then cooked into mush. Hulled corn and dried lima beans was an esteemed dish in South County—a sort of Succotash, you see.

THE SOCIAL CENTER

The fireplace in the early days was not only the focal point for crafts and the center of home work, but it was the social center for the family as well. Women did much of their spinning before the open fire, they heated their tallow for candlemaking, and they boiled their lye for soapmaking at the fireside. There also the men whittled or made objects needed around the house and barn.

During the long winter evenings, for many homes, the firelight was the only light to work by or to play by. This does not mean that there was a complete lack of supplementary light, but fuels such as tallow and grease were conserved as far as possible. Pine knots and splinters tossed on the fire took the place of many a candle.

It was the bright cheerfulness of the fireplace as well as its warmth which made it the natural center of the home. Henry Wadsworth Longfellow, whose poetry described many old customs and places declared that the hanging of the crane in the fireplace of a new home was a rite which established and sanctified the home. He wrote a special poem on the subject "The Hanging of the Crane," from which these stanzas are taken:

THE lights are out, and gone are all the guests

That thronging came with merriment and jests

 To celebrate the Hanging of the Crane

In the new house, — into the night are gone;

But still the fire upon the hearth burns on,

 And I alone remain.

The poem continues:

O fortunate, O happy day
When a new household finds its place
Among the myriad homes of earth,
Like a new star just sprung to birth
And rolled on its harmonious way
Into the boundless realms of space!

And so the guests in speech and song,
As in the chimney burning bright
We hung the iron crane tonight
And merry was the feast and long.

In his poem "Haunted Houses" Longfellow wrote

The stranger at my fireside cannot see
The forms I see, nor hear the sounds I hear,
He but perceives what is, while unto me
All that has been is visible and clear.

It was stated in the introduction that Longfellow once owned and then gave Windmill Cottage, the author's present home, to George Washington Greene and his family. He was a frequent visitor at Windmill Cottage and Professor Greene often visited Longfellow in Cambridge. On one occasion when the poet came to East Greenwich for a wedding he wrote to his friend Mr. J. O. Field and stated,

In one of the rooms was a tea kettle hanging on a crane in the fireplace—so begins a new household.

Of this same wedding, Maude Howe Eliot wrote to the author that she attended the wedding of Rev. Brenton Greene to his cousin Katherine Greene, and that she was accompanied to this wedding at Windmill Cottage by her mother Julia Ward Howe. Sitting around the fireplace with them were "Henry W. Longfellow," Charles Sumner, George Washington Greene and her uncle Samuel Ward.

The role of the fireplace as a social center from the very earliest times has been extolled in poetry and prose which dwells upon its charm, its spiritual values and its romance in addition to its practical uses.

John Greenleaf Whittier's "Snowbound" treats of the fireplace in praise of its warmth and security. Some lines of his poem read:

Shut in from all the world without
We sat the clean winged hearth about
Content to let the north wind roar
In baffled rage at pane and door
While the red logs before us beat
The frost line back with tropic heat.
And ever when a louder blast
Shook beam and rafter as it passed
The merrier up its roaring draught
The great throat of the chimney laughed.
The house dog on his paws out-spread
Laid to the fire his drowsy head.
The cat's dark silhouette on the wall
A couchant tiger's seemed to fall;
And for the winter's fireside meet
Between the andirons straddling feet
The mug of cider simmered slow
The apples sputtered in a row
And, close at hand, the basket stood
With nuts from brown October's wood
What matter how the night behaved?
What matter how the north wind raved?
Blow high, blow low, not all its snow
Could quench our hearth fire's ruddy glow.

Rudyard Kipling wrote the following lines in "The Fires"

How can I turn from any fire
On any man's hearthstone
I know the wonder and desire
That went to build my own.

Christopher Morley wrote a collection of poems entitled "Chimney Smoke" and in so doing helped to perpetuate the nostalgia for fireplaces in three separate poems, one of which is transcribed here:

Do you remember, Heart's Desire,
    The night when Hallowe'en first came?
The newly dedicated fire,
    The hearth unsanctified by flame?

How anxiously we swept the bricks
    (How tragic, were the draught not right!)
And then the blaze enwrapped the sticks
    And filled the room with dancing light.

We could not speak, but only gaze
    Nor half believe what we had seen—
Our home, our hearth, our golden blaze,
    Our cider mugs, our Hallowe'en!

And then a thought occurred to me—

We ran outside with sudden shout
And looked up at the roof, to see
   Our own dear smoke come drifting out.

And of all man's felicities
The very subtlest one, say I,
Is when for the first time he sees
   His hearthfire smoke against the sky.

Not all of the praise of the fireplace was written in poetry. We find in letters and diaries, descriptions and portraits of fireplace living. There are glowing accounts of the sociability and the hospitality which surrounds the early fireplace, so much so that drawings, pictures and stories of today, show the fireplace of yesterday as a thing of romance and charm. A few excerpts or comments in this regard by writers on old time subjects run like this:

The old time kitchen was the real heart of the Country Home of America

Ella Shannon Bowles
in "Homespun Handicrafts"

Wallace Nutting shows a picture in *Furniture Treasury* of decorated culinary articles, utensils such as forks and ladles, and explains that these were usually votive offerings at the shrine of a maiden and hung by her in the fireplace.

Alice Morse Earle in *Home Life in Colonial Days* wrote that the kitchen in all of the farmhouses of all the colonies was the most cheerful, homelike and picturesque room in the house. Indeed it was in town houses as well.

The kitchen had a warm glowing heart that spread light and welcome and made the poor room the home.

Walter A. Dyer in *The Lure of the Antique* wrote that

It is impossible to picture the American Colonist in the 17th and 18th centuries without calling up a vision of the huge kitchen fireplace, with its pewter laden mantle, the old flintlock hung above, strings of peppers and onions overhead. It was a veritable family altar.

Helen Evertson Smith in *Colonial Days and Ways*, wrote:

The great dependence for cheerful light as well as for warmth in winter must have been upon the blazing knots of resinous wood dexterously distributed in among the slower burning logs of hickory, oak and maple. By the blaze of these friendly fires there was seen much domestic happiness and much social enjoyment of a homely sort.

In the *Life and Letters of Horace Bushnell*, published in 1880, he writes of "Home Evening Amusements in Litchfield," ca. 1810–20

But most of all to be remembered are those friendly circles gathered so often round the winter's fire—not the stove, but the fire—the brightly blazing, hospitable fire. In the early dusk, the home circle is drawn more closely and quietly round it; but a good neighbor and his wife drop in shortly from over the way, and the circle begins to spread. Next a few young folk from the other end of the village, entering in brisker mood, find as many more chairs, set in as wedges into the periphery, to receive them also. And then a friendly sleighful of old and young, that have come down from the hill to spend an hour or two; spread the circle again, moving it still farther back from the fire, and the fire blazes just as much higher and more brightly, having a new stick added for every guest. There is no restraint, certainly no affectation of style. They tell stories, they laugh, they sing. They are serious and gay by turns; for the young folks go on with some play, while the fathers and mothers are discussing some hard point of theology in the minister's last sermon; or, perhaps, the great danger coming to sound morals from the multiplication of turnpikes and newspapers! Meantime the good housewife brings out her choice stock of home-grown exotics, gathered from three realms: doughnuts from the pantry, hickory-nuts from the chamber, and the nicest, smoothest apples from the cellar. And then, as the tall clock in the corner of the room ticks on majestically towards nine, the conversation takes, it may be, a little more serious turn, and it is suggested that a very happy evening may fitly be ended with a prayer. Whereupon the circle breaks up with a reverent, congratulative look on every face, which is itself the truest language of a social nature blessed in human fellowship.

In Chapter One of *Old Town Fireside Stories* by Harriet Beecher Stowe one reads

In those days chimney corner story telling became an art and accomplishment. Society then was full of traditions and narratives which had all the uncertain glow and shifting mystery of the firelit hearth upon them. They were told to sympathetic audiences, by the rising and falling light of the solemn embers, with the hearth crickets filling up every pause. Then the aged told their stories to the young, tales of early life.

The "wood spell" was referred to in the chapter on the the "Forest and Wood Fires." Mrs. Harriet Beecher Stowe described such a "spell" in *Old Town Folks*. Her description of the further proceedings after gathering and delivering wood are pertinent to the subject of this chapter:

It was one of the great seasons of preparation in the minister's family and Tina, Harry and I had been busy for 2 or 3 days beforehand in helping Esther create the wood-spell cake, which was to be made in quantities large enough to give ample slices to every parish-ioner. Two days beforehand the fire was besieged with a row of earthen pots in which the spicy compound was rising to the necessary lightness, and Harry and I split incredible amounts of oven wood and in the evening we sat together round the great kitchen fire with Mr. Avery in the midst of us, telling us stories and arguing with us and entering into the hilarity of the thing like a boy.

The minister himself heated two little old irons red-hot in the fire, and therewith from time to time, stirred up a mighty bowl of flip which was to flow in abundance to every comer.

This chapter on the fireplace as a social center brings Part I to conclusion on a happy and romantic note. It is also true that the early Americans who depended upon and also enjoyed their fireplaces had an arduous, hard life. The discipline of living in the pioneer days was rigorous, but the men and women persevered. They built a new country which has made history and is still going forward. The Early American Fireplace contributed significantly to their achievements.

PART II

The Houses

VERMONT FIREPLACE

It was good fortune to come across an early painting of a still earlier Vermont fireplace. The painting is signed, F. H. Shapleigh, 1884, but there is no way to determine the date of the house whose kitchen fireplace is depicted. The artist kept his work simple as regards the utensils and the fireplace room itself. A crane and andirons have their place, and tongs and a shovel or peel are leaning in the corner at the right.

A country chair, a hutch chair-table and a basket are the only room furnishings. The wide floorboards and the two panelled doors are typical of an old farm house. The wooden lintel projects enough to serve as a mantel. The brick oven is arched at the top and has an iron door. Below is the ash well.

It is unusual to find a fireplace with the brickwork exposed on the first floor as the chimney narrows on its upward course. The space provides "cubby holes" instead of cupboards, in which are shown two pewter candlesticks on the left and two "sad" irons on the right-hand side. Several pieces of pewter rest on the mantel. Above the fireplace is a drying pole suspended from the ceiling by hooks.

The painting, which brought a very good price, was sold at auction in May, 1970.

THE LONGFELLOW HOUSE
Cambridge, Massachusetts

The "study" fireplace at the Longfellow House, sometimes called Craigie House, is included in the group of fireplace illustrations, especially because of its relationship to the poet Henry Wadsworth Longfellow. He owned, for a short time, the Windmill Cottage, now owned and occupied by the author. A photograph of its fireplace at Christmastime is shown as the frontispiece.

Mr. Longfellow is shown during the latter part of his life, seated by the fire in his study. The house is a stately wooden structure on Brattle Street in Cambridge. Mr. Thomas H. de Valcourt, curator of The Longfellow House, wrote that "Mr. Longfellow had this fireplace converted to burning channel coal in 1846," which is the reason for the grate in the fireplace.

A bust of George Washington Greene cannot be seen but is in this study. It was to Professor Greene and his family that Longfellow, a lifelong friend, gave Windmill Cottage in East Greenwich, Rhode Island.

The fireplace wall has attractive paneling in this high ceilinged room and in the center panel over the mantel a fine Girondelle mirror is placed. In front on the hearth of the fireplace is a substantial and long fender with three brass ball finials along its top.

THE OLD SMITH HOUSE
Saxton's River, Vermont

The author visited Saxton's River to speak before the Historical Society on "Early Fireplaces" and had the unique experience, to him, of seeing a "soapstone" fireplace through the courtesy of Mrs. Lawrence M. Moore, a daughter of the owner-occupants, who were away. Although she has not been able to find the date when the house was built, Mrs. Moore has provided the following report on the house and fireplace:

Soapstone fireplace and brick oven at the 5th generation home of Mr. and Mrs. Humphrey Bancroft Neill in Saxton's River, Vermont. Mr. Neill's grandmother is demonstrating how her mother used to bake pies in the brick oven. (The turkey will be cooked in a tin oven in the fireplace.)

Mr. Neill's great-grandfather, Benjamin Smith, brought his family to live in this house in 1828. At that time, Mr. Smith was engaged in the soapstone business, quarrying the stone near Saxton's River and bringing it down the mountainside with oxen to his finishing mills where it was made into sinks, stoves, parts of fireplaces, and other products.

Actually, the soapstone, in this case, is constructed as a veneer and mantelpiece over a much earlier brick fireplace. The veneer does not extend to the brick oven and ash storage space which are closed over by an original paneled door when shut. The original hearth has been replaced with soapstone squares. Thus, we see a native industry expressing itself, just as granite did, especially in Connecticut, in serving for hearths, lintels and even jambs.

THE PRENTIS ROOMS

Concord, New Hampshire

This kitchen fireplace in one of the Prentis rooms in the New Hampshire Historical Society is included as a fine example of a re-created fireplace and because of the quality of the furnishings.

The rooms are intended to suggest the home of a prosperous merchant around the year 1730. The furnishings include heirlooms; many were hand made in the home during the owner's lifetime and generally represent the period from 1680 to 1730. The kitchen was built around the fireplace paneling and the old feather edged panels above it.

The fireplace was copied from one in Henniker, N. H., and the two panels above it came from an old New Hampshire house.

A complete clock jack and spit are installed at the fireplace. Some of the other typical and unusual articles of equipment are a candle-holding rush holder, a pair of early brass candlesticks, an hourglass and two pieces of slipware. Skilled blacksmith artisans produced the decorative griddle, toaster, fork and the heart-shaped trivet leaning on the brick oven shelf. A rare double boiler hangs from the crane, and at the left is a toasting or broiling rack. Two pots of bell metal rest on the hearth and a very unusual spatula hangs from the mantel shelf. Other items include a tobacco and pipe box, a hanging rack for small utensils, a skewer holder and skewers, bellows and an old flintlock musket. The iron andirons are brass-headed and have a series of three spit racks on the front columns. The ever-present teakettle hangs from the crane.

Courtesy of New Hampshire Historical Society

Photos Courtesy Phelps Studio, Henniker, N.H.

FRANKLIN PIERCE HOMESTEAD
Hillsboro, New Hampshire

A National Historic Landmark, this house was built in 1804 by the father of Franklin Pierce, the 14th President of the United States. The father, Benjamin Pierce, was a two-time Governor of New Hampshire. The homestead is maintained by the State and was completely restored in 1957 to reflect the 1804–39 period when the younger Pierce lived at home.

The three photos show features of the restoration as it was taking place and illustrate what many historic houses have gone through to bring them back to their original state:

The kitchen fireplace

The East front room behind the kitchen; close-up showing inner brick work

The Ballroom Fireplace

THE CHASE HOUSE

Strawbery Banke, Portsmouth, New Hampshire

A mid-Georgian Mansion built in 1762 by mariner John Underwood of Kittery. Stephen Chase purchased the house in 1799 after having lived in it for some years.

Stephen Chase entertained President George Washington in this house at an evening reception during the newly elected President's triumphal tour of the colonies in 1789.

Architecturally, the Chase House is one of the richest dwellings of its size in Portsmouth.

The fireplace shown here is in the eastern front room, which has window seats, sliding shutters, wainscoting and a lovely mantelpiece, which are thought not to have been finished until after the Revolution. The fireplace frieze, elaborately carved from white pine, has the intricate "Tudor Rose" pattern.

This fireplace is shown here as another example of a "parlor" fireplace, in a patrician's or well-to-do owner's home. It is decorative as well as practical and has brass furnishings—andirons and fender—which go with an elegant home in an important Colonial seaport.

THE JEHIEL WEBB HOUSE
Rockingham, Vermont

The house was built about 1766 by David Pulsifer, who ran the house as an Inn. After the battle of Lexington, he went off to war and never returned. The Inn was taken over by Jehiel Webb who gave the house its name.

Mr. Robert Avery Smith, the present owner, says of the fireplace and keeping room,

The paneling and paint (red) are original. The iron scoop in the fireplace is from an old house in the area. The crane is original. The peel and the kettle are Vermont items and the hanging grill is an early New England piece, the bellows have the old decoration on them. An early American footed pan is in the ash "box". The sconces are Early 19th Century. The pitcher (in the brick oven) is probably Bennington (Vt.) The iron andirons are like those found in this area with looped necks.

The photo also shows a loom basket hanging on the sheathing, at the right, and at the far left a lanthorn. The tub or large basket on the hearth is made of birch bark with rawhide binding and handle across the top (probably Indian).

The lintel is stone and the stone is worn on the left side from sharpening knives over the years. The fireplace and brick oven together measure eight feet four inches. The height is fifty inches. The brick oven has a separate flue. The bricks on the hearth were laid in sand, and the hearth is twelve feet long by three feet six inches wide.

The Jehiel Webb House, when an Inn, was famous as a stage coach stopover on the Boston to Rutland route.

76

CAPTAIN JOHN CLARK HOUSE

Strawbery Banke, Portsmouth, New Hampshire

Colonists settled Portsmouth at Strawbery Banke in 1630. The settlement was renamed Portsmouth in 1653.

The Capt. John Clark House was built in 1750. It was purchased by Captain Clark, a packet-master in 1839, after having lived in it from 1834. The Clark Family which gave the house its name, lived here from 1834 to 1874.

Inside, the Clark House is notable for an unusual mixture of simplicity and elegance and for the abundance of its paneling. The central brick chimney contains many green glazed bricks, which are thought to have been manufactured in the area.

The fireplace hearth is made of large oblong bricks with an outer row of square bricks. The brick oven is in the upper back corner on the left. A special feature is the very high mantel shelf leaving little overmantel space, but below which is simple but beautiful paneling. The cupboard with its fine pewter adds to the attractiveness of the room. Several early lighting devices hang from the mantel and a number of tools and utensils add to the old time atmosphere, to include a peel, a long-handled skillet, toaster, roasting oven, griddle, kettles, tongs and an iron-handled warming pan.

Courtesy of Strawbery Banke, Inc.

DANIEL WEBSTER HOMESTEAD
Franklin, New Hampshire

The birthplace and boyhood home of Daniel Webster, the formidable anti-slavery Senator who was an orator, Congressman from New Hampshire, and twice Secretary of State. The house of two rooms was built around 1780. It is now a State historic site maintained by the State of New Hampshire.

The house is a primitive one, and the interesting fireplace dominates the larger of two small rooms. The small closet in the overmantel space is called a Bible closet. On the thin mantel shelf are several small items which include a runlet, a mortar and pestle and a candle mold. In the fireplace and on the hearth are usual items pertaining to an early fireplace such as pans and kettles, a foot warmer and warming pan, a large tin roasting oven and a wrought iron oven peel. The doors to the oven and ash well are cast iron and on hinges. The niche or opening in the brickwork on the left could have been used as a place in which to keep things dry.

OLD GAOL MUSEUM
York, Maine

The Old Gaol was built in 1653 as The King's Prison and is the oldest existing English public building in America. It operates now as a museum and is noted for its dungeons and collections of ironware, furniture and china.

It was not unusual in those days for the jailkeeper or sheriff and his family to have quarters in the same building with the "Gaol". The Historical Society in Kingston, R. I. occupies a jailkeeper's house which has family rooms in the front part on two floors with the jail cells behind and below.

The fine old fireplace in the Old Gaol was for the use of the jailkeeper's family. It was their kitchen fireplace. On a thin projecting shelf above the lintel (which serves as a mantel), and hanging from it, the Museum's

collection of lighting devices is displayed. These are especially noticeable to the author, who collects lighting devices as well as fireplace utensils.

The brick oven is an excellent example of one with an inner brick "frame" against which an oven door would be placed during the baking process. On the hearth and in the fireplace itself a good assortment of fireplace hardware is shown. This exhibit is dominated by the roasting oven or tin kitchen.

Poles suspended from the ceiling by hooks were used for drying foods, herbs and clothing. At the left of the picture, some old-time kitchen furniture can be seen, at least partially: a table dough box, a cheese press, a cheese basket, a pewter candle mold, butter scales and a stencilled tray.

Courtesy, Old Gaol Museum

THE HITCHCOCK HOUSE

Putney, Vermont

This Vermont village fireplace is typical of many in northern New England. It is an original fireplace in a restored house. The niche over the narrow mantel runs the full length of the lintel, and it may have had a door or doors at one time and served as a shallow closet. Now, however, it is a fine display case for the pewter pieces in it. In this picture we see the reel and flax wheel which were often used near the fireplace. Some homespun is draped over a tip table, and pewter dishes, teapot and candlestick are on a butterfly table. A "hog scraper" candlestick is hung on the slat of a ladderback chair, by a lip on the candlestick, as in the days of yore.

Elsewhere around the fireplace are kettles hanging from the crane, a long handled frying pan, a three legged skillet and pot, and a tailor's goose on the hearth, a griddle, bellows and wooden ware hanging from the lintel—and leaning against the brickwork by the brick oven are several peels.

The bricks used for this fireplace show clearly their home-made character. An unusual feature is a wooden "lintel" inserted in the brickwork at the top of the ash storage space.

Two photographs show this fireplace, not in the process of restoration, but rather in the process of "discovery". The fireplace had been closed with the advent of stoves. The front of the fireplace had been bricked up and then plastered over. The front of the bake oven and ash storage box also had been bricked up and they had a wooden door cover. A pile of bricks and plaster are to be seen in the foreground, which for a long time had concealed the fireplace.

"In the process of discovery"

Courtesy of Mrs. Arthur C. Hitchcock

THE JOSHUA GEORGE HOMESTEAD
Warner, New Hampshire

There is no exact date, but the present occupant, a descendant of the builder-owner, says "it was probably built before 1800."

The two-story hip-roofed house has two chimneys and four fireplaces. One room in a large ell served as a kitchen-dining room. At the big fireplace in this room, all the cooking was done in the brick oven, on the crane, or in front of the fire.

In 1928, a complete Thanksgiving dinner for twelve was entirely cooked, using this fireplace, with the turkey in the tin roasting oven on the hearth, the vegetables in pots on the crane, the pies and puddings in the brick oven.

It will be noted that the oven is recessed or set back in the brickwork. This probably means that the fireplace flue served as an oven flue. A handy shelf was provided by this construction.

A fine array of pewter is spread out on the mantelpiece. The rounded part of the jambs are not original. They were made of maple bedposts, sawed lengthwise and overlaid on the jambs.

The house is now owned by Nancy Sibley Wilkins, a great granddaughter of Joshua George.

Courtesy of Harlow Old Fort House

GREAT FIREPLACE, HARLOW OLD FORT HOUSE
Plymouth, Massachusetts

The house is maintained by the Plymouth Antiquarian Society. It dates from 1677. The fireplace is called the Great Fireplace—the name might well apply to quite a number of large fireplaces which served the kitchen-keeping room.

At one side, in front of the fireplace a woman in Pilgrim garb is shown taking her bread out of the brick oven with a wooden peel. The fire hazard of having the oven in back and behind the fireplace can be appreciated from this picture, for in the early days huge logs were put in the chimney place, and the fire was spread well across the entire space.

A few items which we have not seen often or at all, in the other fireplace illustrations are the bean pot, a brass kettle on the rim of a long legged trivet, a clay pipe in the pipe and tobacco box, a wooden spill box just above the massive oak lintel and a spit rod behind the box. This type of spit bar or rod is placed on andiron hangers, but none show in the picture. A wooden oven door is on the hearth below the oven. The pot and skillet hang from a lug pole up in the chimney throat. A very fine primitive candle stand is at the very left, behind the housewife.

THE IRONMASTER'S HOUSE

Saugus Iron Works, Saugus, Massachusetts

The Ironmaster's House is on the "grounds" and is an integral part of the Iron Works.* It is the only unit which did not require restoration and stands today, as it did originally, on a bank above the re-created Iron Works Industry.

The Saugus Iron Works dates from 1650 and included with this date must be the house and its keeping room fireplace which is also the kitchen fireplace.

The fireplace utensils are numerous. Here we find the wooden crane above the lintel on which herbs are hung for drying. Herbs were used for flavoring and for medicinal purposes. A lug pole trammel holds a kettle, behind which on the back wall is a fireback which was made in 1655 at Kittery, Maine.† There are two ovens and a shelf on each side on which to rest cooking and heating utensils. A number of items hang from or on the lintel, including a musket and powder horn, boots and a boot jack, a toaster and wooden dipper, tongs and steelyards. A child's rocking chair is on the hearth, and in the foreground is a deer skin rug and a candle stand. A mortar and pestle stands on a bench and another one on a fireplace shelf.

* The Saugus Iron Works became a National Historic Site on June 21, 1969 as the birthplace of the 319 year old American Iron and Steel Industry.

† Information from "100 Most Beautiful Rooms in America" by Helen Comstock.

Photograph by Samuel Chamberlain

Photograph by William B. Keefe

BALCH HOUSE

Beverly, Massachusetts

The Beverly Historical Society now maintains that the Balch House is the oldest house still standing in the United States. Their brochure says "it is positively established as the oldest house." The structure was built in the spring of 1636. Time has brought many changes, and the present structure is far from the original two story design; e.g., in 1650 an extension was built on the south side of the original house with a chimney between.

"The fireplace is original and complete with oven" yet it is of the size, and has the oven placement of a later period than the house itself; for example, the opening of the brick oven and the ash storage space are in the face of the brick outside of the chimney place. This development came about generally at the same time the fireplaces were reduced in size. One change led to the other. It is possible, therefore, that a fireplace behind this

fireplace might be found should exploration be made.

Exhibited in and around the fireplace are quite a number of primitive and pioneer utensils. There are two muskets, one of which hangs above the mantel. On the mantel can be seen a couple of tin tea caddies, a tin box, a tinder box, and a two tube candle mold. The oven now has a nursery lamp in the opening and a coal carrier hanging alongside. The powder horn hangs on a panel which is just over the lintel and under the unusually high mantel. The hearth contains an old roasting oven, an oven peel, kettle and pots, two foot warmers and what appears to be a mechanical butter churn. The ceiling beams are exposed, and there is vertical sheathing at the right of the fireplace. A pine kitchen table against the sheathing has an iron, a pottery milk crock and a bread basket on

it, while underneath is a dough box. Dough boxes are more numerous in Pennsylvania than New England. A whale oil lantern hangs from a beam and a brass ladle, a sap yoke and a large wooden bowl are hung on the sheathing. A wall coffee grinder is attached to the wall at the left end of the table.

It will be noted that an open door at the left side will, when shut, enclose the brick oven and the brick work below it.

HOPKINS HOUSE

Plimoth Plantations, Plymouth, Massachusetts

Plimoth Plantations is a re-creation of the first settlement of the Pilgrims in Plymouth, Massachusetts, where they landed in 1620. The fireplace shown here is in the Hopkins House which is the most recently completed and "as far as can be determined the most architecturally correct house at the Plantation."

The fireplace furnishings are very simple, no doubt to be as exact as possible in showing the necessary but all too few pots and pans which were brought to our shores by the same ship which brought the settlers themselves. Included among the vessels are two brass kettles, a small cauldron hanging on one of the lug pole trammels, a large frying pan with a medium length handle and a covered pot. In the corner by the left jamb is a copper warming pan with a wrought iron handle. No illuminant is to be seen except the fire in the fireplace. A simple bake house may have been attached but "outdoors." The fire is built on very small "firedogs" so that it is hardly above the stone floor of the Chimney Place. Note that the oak jambs give the main support to the lintel rather than the stone work doing so.

The hearth is built of many stones mortared together. It was later that granite quarries were opened up, and single slabs made a hearthstone. The huge pieces of granite must have been hauled by oxen.

Courtesy of Plimoth Plantation

Courtesy of Old Sturbridge Village

PLINY FREEMAN FARM HOUSE

Old Sturbridge Village, Sturbridge, Massachusetts

An 18th century farmhouse which was moved with its outbuildings from Sturbridge. The farm has the objective of recreating life on a small New England farm of the early 1800's. The farmer's wife baked bread, beans and gingerbread in her brick oven. Among other things, stews, soups and puddings were cooked over the open fire in the kitchen fireplace, which is shown here.

The utensils displayed in this fireplace include a tobacco box and tongs on the right jamb and a large wooden peel on the left jamb. A large three-legged kettle with cover sits on the hearth, as do a spider, toaster, trivet and Dutch oven. The narrow mantel contains a noggin or wooden pitcher, an iron, pewter charger (plate), candle mold, two pewter mugs, a small brush, a tinder box, four "hog scraper" candle holders and a tea canister. The bellows behind the Old Sturbridge made broom has an unusually long "nozzle."

STEPHEN FITCH HOUSE

Old Sturbridge Village, Sturbridge, Massachusetts

The Fitch house was moved to Old Sturbridge from Willimantic, Connecticut. It is a half-gambrel-roofed house which was built in 1735. The Village leaflet says, "It reflects the plain dignity of farm homes around which the New England Community was built." Candle dipping and candle molding are demonstrated at a summer kitchen fireplace in the same house.

Here is an excellent example of the stone fireplace. The lintel, jamb, hearth and in fact the walls of the fireplace are all stone. What appears to be three ovens, in fact, is only one oven at the top, below which are two open storage areas, one of which no doubt was used for ashes. These areas are made of brick which is more adaptable for use in smaller spaces. An open door at the right of the fireplace can be used to enclose the entire right side.

The accessories include: on the left side, a pipe and tobacco box, a heart shaped trivet, a waffle iron and tongs; on the right wall, vertical to the fireplace stands a peel against the "door" and hanging is a skimmer, a long handled dipper and a wooden peel (almost out of the picture). On the hearth is a three-legged pot and a kettle resting on a trivet, while in the fireplace hanging from the crane is a kettle and a skillet. Overhead on the mantel are a pewter tea pot and charger, two irons, a tinder box and candlestick while a cruisie or wick channel lamp hangs from a saw tooth trammel.

Courtesy of Old Sturbridge Village

THE CAPTAIN ANDREW FULLER HOUSE

Middleton, Massachusetts,

privately owned by Mrs. Charles H. Watkins

In this house is one of the finest examples of an early American fireplace. It is notable for its two brick ovens, both within the fireplace opening in the back wall.

Mrs. Watkins writes of her fireplace,

There are two ovens which originally had metal doors with handles. The opening at the lower left is an ash pit five feet deep. This fireplace is original except the right end where a later oven had been built in front of the old one.

A new lintel had to be put in place as the whole (front) was supported on brickwork before we opened it up. This was cut from a red oak tree and hewn by hand to the original form. The kettles hung from a lug pole. The sockets of the original lug pole corners were found during the work of restoration. At a later period there was a long crane—the crane eyes are still there.

The front of the hearth probably had originally square tiles—they appear in other fireplaces here.

There is

a ledge running across the back wall of the fireplace. This was to accommodate the oven doors, which the housewife could use when she opened the oven door by just sliding the door along.

Of the utensils, the long handled frying

90

pan or skillet is of special interest as is the warming pan which has a wrought iron handle and is older and rarer than those with a wooden handle. An earthenware dye pot with a glazed interior is next to the frying pan at the right.

THE THOMAS HART HOUSE
Metropolitan Museum of Art, New York City

The fireplace in the Thomas Hart House was built about 1640 in Ipswich, Massachusetts. It is now in the American Wing of the Metropolitan Museum of Art.

This fireplace is included among the illustrations primarily because of its construction. It will be noted that the sides and back form a curve, or rounded shape as they come together, and the brick oven is in the "curve" instead of a flat back or side wall.

Here too we find vertical sheathing and very wide floor boards in front of the hearth. The andirons with spit hooks at different levels are interesting. A cruisie or grease lamp hangs in front of the right hand jamb, and a wrought iron handled warming pan leans against the left jamb. The kettle is suspended by an adjustable peg and hole trammel.

The fireplace room is here called the "keeping room". The room besides the sheathing, contains "summer" beams, girts, corner posts and casements.

Courtesy of the Metropolitan Museum of Art, New York

Courtesy of Braintree Historical Society

THE GENERAL SYLVANUS THAYER BIRTHPLACE
South Braintree, Massachusetts

The house was erected in 1720 by the great-great-grandfather of Sylvanus Thayer, and the original structure is still in good condition. General Thayer is noted as the "father" of the U. S. Military Academy at West Point.

Two views of the fireplace are shown. It is a stone fireplace including the hearth, but the oven has a brick face and brick interior which is seen in the upper photo. This view also shows an iron bar inside the fireplace opening, on which small utensils are hung. Both horizontal and vertical sheathing is used around the fireplace which dresses it up very well.

A very large wooden oven peel hangs along the left jamb, and the tin kitchen is placed before the fire where it normally would be used.

The lower view shows how dipped candles were often dried—on rods between two chairs. A brass kettle full of tallow is alongside on a stool.

A feature of the house itself is a sunken buttery recently discovered under a modern pantry. It has a brick floor, two granite steps leading down to it, and a large brick trough for holding ice and milk, etc.

92

FAIRBANKS HOUSE

Dedham, Massachusetts

Built in 1636, the same year that Harvard College was founded, the Fairbanks House is the nation's oldest * wood-frame house. It is a registered National Landmark, spectacular partly because it is in its original condition—wholly unrestored. Eight generations of Fairbanks have lived in the house continuously until 1903 when the Fairbanks Family in America was created to maintain the home within the family and to receive memorabilia returned to the homestead.

The fireplace in the home is not huge,

* The Architectural Department of the Boston Public Library has reported the Fairbanks House to be the oldest.

which leads one to suspect that if restoration took place a larger fireplace behind this one might be found. The lintel is one which goes with a very large fireplace. Here are seen a sawtooth trammel which was used with a lug pole and a number of utensils common to an early fireplace including two sizes of griddles, two toasters, a boot jack leaning against the jamb under an oven peel. A foot warmer is on a stool, and a kettle hangs from a crane by an adjustable peg and hole trammel. No doubt the crane was installed when the size of the fireplace was reduced—which is a supposition on the part of the author.

WHITEHALL

Middletown, Rhode Island

Here we have the fine old kitchen fireplace in the Bishop Berkeley House. The parlor fireplace is shown elsewhere among the illustrations.

The lintel is massive, the fireplace is wide and high, the bake oven is in the back wall and it is well furnished with "hardware" of the period.

There are two "tin kitchens" * of slightly different size. The rather tall andirons have a spit rack on the front of the columns.

* The author often has referred to the roasting oven as a tin kitchen, which name he happens to like, but one will often find it called a reflector oven.

A very rare double bellows rests on the hearth. The only other one the author knows about is in his collection—a recent acquisition.

A lantern, mortar and pestle, candle molds, pipe tongs hanging from the lintel, a toaster, butter churn, pots and kettles and a few small utensils complete the picture.

The house was built in 1729. Bishop George Berkeley was a noted English philosopher.

Mrs. Henry W. Whitney writes that the fireplace in the cellar of the house was used by Berkeley's slaves undoubtedly, as pallets were found there.

Courtesy of Providence Journal Company

Courtesy of the Rhode Island Pendulum *and Mrs. Amos Hazard*

THE "BROWNBREAD" HOUSE

East Greenwich, Rhode Island

Located on Middle Road and built in 1710, the so-called Brownbread House is owned privately by Mrs. Amos Hazard. The house has a central chimney with five fireplaces. The fireplace shown is considered to be the kitchen fireplace. However, there is a large stone fireplace in the basement, perhaps a scullery, which measures nine feet in width and five feet in height. Each of these two fireplaces has a beehive oven. A warming oven, an unusual feature, was built over the beehive oven on the first floor. The opening to the warming oven is from the room behind the baking oven and fireplace, which is used as a dining room. Under the brick oven is a larger than usual ash well, which could have been used also to keep the "oven wood" between bakings.

The cobbler's bench in the foreground makes a convenient stool and provides atmosphere and who can say that some shoes were not cobbled in front of the fireplace.

The History of East Greenwich, R. I. by Martha McPartland reads,

Tradition says that the name Brownbread House came from the fact that on Saturday nights beans were cooked at the other Spencer house called Lilac Cottage and the brownbread was cooked here. The Spencer families suppered on alternate Saturday nights at the Lilac Cottage and Brownbread Place.

JOSEPH REYNOLDS HOUSE
Bristol, Rhode Island

The fireplace and fireplace wall in the "keeping" room of the Joseph Reynolds House in Bristol built in 1698. This house served as the Bristol headquarters of General Lafayette.

Mrs. Antoinette Downing wrote that the building was unusually large for the period—also quite pretentious. The house has two brick chimneys built on the inside walls of the house, each of which contains a large fireplace. In this picture of the "keeping" room fireplace, the overmantel and the whole "fireplace wall" is paneled with bolection paneling. It is an important early example of the use of paneling and is evidence of the change of style taking place at the end of the seventeenth century. The crane in the fireplace extends almost to the opposite side and a fender about a foot high stretches across the entire front. The screen inside may furnish added protection from sparks, but it does not belong. Neither does the wood in the cradle, which reminds one that today's fireplace enthusiasts use cradles and brass kettles for wood boxes—desecration, yes—but they are supposed to add atmosphere.

As shown in the photograph the paneling was marbled. The original wall finish has now been painted over.

Courtesy of Rhode Island Development Council

NICHOLAS-WANTON-HUNTER HOUSE
Newport, Rhode Island

This volume on Early Fireplaces is devoted chiefly to the kitchen fireplace as the center of the household, but the more elegant house is illustrated several times to show a type without which no book on fireplaces would be complete. The Hunter House fireplace is such an example.

This house, one of the finest in Newport, was built in 1746 by Jonathan Nichols, a Newport merchant, who became a Deputy Governor.

The interior of the house is noted for its fine woodwork, and this parlor fireplace exhibits lovely horizontal panels in the overmantel space, two pilasters, one at each side, and identical china cupboards on each side.

The fireplace itself has a marble face and hearth, and before it on the hearth is a fire screen and an adjustable floor candle stand. Over the fireplace at each side is a candle sconce with a "hurricane" chimney.

"WHITEHALL"

Middletown, Rhode Island

The rich paneling and Delft tile are principal features of the attractive study and fireplace in the Bishop George Berkeley House called "Whitehall." The house was built in 1729 by Bishop Berkeley, and it was here that he wrote the poem containing the line, "Westward the course of empire makes its way."

This is a beautiful parlor fireplace in an elegant home. Even the door has paneling in keeping with the rest of the wall. Here we have the brass bucket (used as a wood box) and the most common type of foot warmer which might have been taken to church in the sleigh.

One of the panels—seen over the chair—seems to be a door to a "secret" closet and has a small key hole near the edge.

Whitehall also has a very fine and notable kitchen fireplace which is included among the illustrations.

GOVERNOR WILLIAM GREENE HOUSE
Warwick, Rhode Island

Built in 1680, the original farmhouse consisted of two rooms on the first floor and two on the second. These rooms were built against a large stone chimney which covered the entire west end of the house. The Greene family began ownership in 1718. William Greene Jr., who inherited the house in 1758, served as Governor of Rhode Island. The Greenes were good friends of Benjamin Franklin who visited the farm often. The property is now owned by Mrs. William Greene Roelker Jr. The house is practically a manor house, having been added to from time to time.

The fireplace is an enormous one, in which a settle is placed at one end. In the right back corner is the brick oven, while a hob or shelf is in the opposite corner. The fireplace has huge brass andirons which are in keeping with its size, and the small fender posts can be seen on the arms of the andirons.

Brass utensils are the rule, one of which is a fine plate warmer. The brass bellows are unusual. A brass water kettle has been put in the oven opening, and an old flintlock gun adorns the lintel as it probably did in the days of the Indians.

Courtesy of Mrs. William Greene Roelker, Jr.; Photographer, Thomas Stevens

Courtesy of The Varnum Continentals

THE VARNUM HOUSE

East Greenwich, Rhode Island

Some houses are historic because of who built or lived in them. Such a house is the Varnum House. In 1773 James Mitchell Varnum "built a mansion in keeping with the best architectural standards of the time." James Varnum was the first commander of the Kentish Guards with the rank of Colonel. In 1777 he was commissioned Brigadier General in the Continental Army and served with distinction in a number of engagements. He also was an attorney of prominence in his day.

The kitchen fireplace shown here has been restored to its original state. There is no evidence of a brick oven. This makes it seem probable that there was a bake house as an outbuilding, which is known to be the case at the Dr. Eldredge House nearby.

The House is maintained as a Museum by the Varnum Continentals.

Some of the equipment exhibited includes a copper kettle on the hearth, and a copper hot water kettle hanging from the crane next to a cast iron tea kettle. The pair of andirons have a heart in the columns near the top, no doubt made by a sentimental blacksmith. The doorless cupboard in the overmantel makes an excellent display space, and the two symmetrically placed panels make attractive locations for the candle sconces.

Courtesy of Mrs. George E. Downing

JOHN TRIPP HOUSE
Manton, Rhode Island

A small house of two rooms on the first floor was built about 1725. A square section of the stone chimney which is topped with brick is left exposed to view. The oven built into the back side of the fireplace extends beyond the chimney, outside the house, in the beehive form which is now quite rare. The oven is made of stone covered with clam shells in plaster.

The lintel holds a narrow mantel above which is beveled paneling. The nearby doors are sheathed. A small niche appears in the brickwork at the right hand side of the fireplace—probably used to keep tobacco in.

The fireplace abuts a wall on one side, which is not uncommon. The open niche in the brick is uncommon, and the oven is unusual although in this side view the opening does not show. The furnishings and furniture are of later periods.

Since this photograph was taken, the house has been moved to Newport, R. I. It now stands on Washington St.

ISRAEL ARNOLD HOUSE

Lincoln, Rhode Island

The early part of this dwelling was a one-room gambrel roofed house with an exposed end chimney of brick. It was built around 1720 to 1725 and passed into Arnold hands by marriage. An addition in the form of a two story center chimney house took place sometime before 1776. The "kitchen" fireplace is 10 feet 4 inches across and 3 feet 9 inches high. The "shallow" mantel over the lintel is finished by a classic molding. The oven opening is a dome or arch shape at the top.

An early warming pan hangs from the left jamb and an oven peel stands by the oven.

The crane holds pots, hooks and a brass kettle while the mantel shows off a number of lighting devices—mostly of a much later period than the fireplace itself. A musket and powder horn are located in the overmantel. A very long fork rests against the right side of the fireplace. Braided scatter rugs are on the floor in front of the hearth and the doors on either side.

At the right of the fireplace is a narrow door which leads to a smoke house behind the chimney where hams were smoked.

Courtesy of Mrs. George E. Downing

Courtesy of Rhode Island Development Council

SMITH'S CASTLE OR COCUMSCUSSOC
Wickford, Rhode Island

In the days of Indian massacres a large, fortified dwelling was called a castle. Smith's Castle was built in 1678. On the grounds is the mass grave of 40 Colonial soldiers killed in 1675, in the Great Swamp Fight with the Indians.

The fireplace is eight feet wide and five and a half feet high. The brick oven is almost directly behind the fire logs. A small recessed place or nook above the lintel affords a place in which to keep materials dry, which dampness would injure.

A pair of bellows hangs on the left jamb, and a tin kitchen oven is on the hearth behind the bench. The wing chair which is made entirely of wood has sides like a settle to protect the user from draughts.

Mr. John W. Haley wrote about this fireplace as follows:

> The owner wishing to bring the original fireplace to light, for it had long been closed, set men at work unbricking it. They opened the fireplace, but it was not the original fireplace, for a second one back of the first was revealed. Back of the second they found still a third hearth, presumably the original one.

A report in 1970 of the Golden Ball Tavern restoration in Weston, Massachusetts reads,

> On the first floor of the southwest room of the Tavern, it was evident that the old fireplace was not the original one. As a matter of exploration, we removed a few bricks in two places. About a foot behind the fireplace is the original and larger fireplace. By building the newer (1800?) fireplace out further into the room, they had developed what one might call the country cousin of the Franklin Stove.

GILBERT STUART BIRTHPLACE

North Kingston, Rhode Island

The home where Gilbert Stuart was born was built in 1751. Stuart was the foremost painter of portraits of George Washington. The view shown above is the living room, which has a corner fireplace. There were quite a number of early fireplaces built in the corner of a room. Another one is in the Dutch House in New Castle, Delaware. Other examples are the Richard Brown House in Providence and the Caleb Daggett House in Newport, R. I.

The kitchen oven and fireplace on the first floor, shown below, occupy a large part of an entire brick wall. This fireplace has an oak lintel, and the overmantel space is exposed brick work, whereas the living room fireplace has vertical sheathing around it with a cupboard on one side and a door to a narrow stairway on the other side.

PUTNAM COTTAGE
Greenwich, Connecticut

General Israel Putnam, who served under George Washington during the American Revolution used Putnam Cottage as his headquarters when it was Knapp's Tavern. In 1814, the Tavern was acquired by a Dr. Tracy and during the occupancy of his family it was remodeled in a Victorian manner. The fireplaces, of which there are six, were bricked in, but the original old panelling was left intact.

A real treasure was uncovered very recently when the restoration of a room was underway. Behind a relatively contemporary fireplace, the original fine old fieldstone fireplace was found. The lintel, some of which shows in the photograph is a huge hand cut oak beam. The bake oven, in the back wall of the chimney place, measures 26 inches deep, 18 inches wide and 24 inches tall at the front. Even the arch of the oven front is made of irregular fieldstone.

The central chimney which supports the six fireplaces, only one of which has been uncovered so far, has a foundation base 20 by 20 feet.

Putnam Cottage is maintained by the Putnam Hill Chapter D.A.R. Already early fireplace equipment and utensils have been assembled and displayed. They make the huge fireplace more of a reality. A pot hangs from the old crane and on the hearth or fireplace floor are exhibited a cast iron tea kettle, a toaster, a hanging skillet, griddle, brass bucket, flax wheel and warming pan, in addition to the small andirons.

THE CAPTAIN JOHN KNAP HOUSE
Stamford, Connecticut

The Knap House is the oldest house being lived in in Stamford, although the Historical Society owns a slightly older house. The Knap House has been traced back to Capt. Knap who would have built it about 1712.

The native stone central chimney which supports the fireplaces is 12 feet square at the base and is original all the way to the top.

This keeping room fireplace is perhaps the widest fireplace in New England. The width of the opening is 10 feet, 4 inches and the height is 5 feet, 4 inches. There is now an additional 6½ inch lintel which is very old and is still in place. It is thought to have been added to improve the draft. This addition to the lintel can be seen in the photograph.

The fireplace, which is made of native fieldstone, is wide enough for a substantial fire to be built in one end of it, freeing the oven for use with greater ease and safety.

The bake oven has a stone floor and a brick beehive dome.

Quite a number of items, which are associated with a fireplace such as this, are shown, including a kettle, toaster and peel on the hearth, a chestnut roaster, fork and measure hanging from the lintel at the right and a group of small implements on a rack at the left end of the lintel. The lintel also holds a betty lamp, a flint lock gun and powder horn. A pipe and tobacco box is shown at the extreme left on the sheathing.

The Knap House, used as a residence, is owned by Mr. Robert Davis.

106

Courtesy of Robert Davis

THE CAPTAIN JOHN KNAP HOUSE

Stamford, Connecticut

The keeping room fireplace in the Knap House is separately illustrated and described. The sitting room fireplace is shown here in addition, because of special features which will be pointed out.

This fireplace, built around 1712, was faced * some time in the 19th Century and the present owner occupant, Mr. Robert Davis,

has kept it in this state "as an interesting example of beautification". A rather large parson's cupboard is at the left of the fireplace. Such a cupboard in the Daniel Webster birthplace is above the fireplace, in the over mantel space.

The principal feature of this fireplace is the bolection molding framing it, which is unique as the largest example in existence—at least so far as now known.

This bolection molding has as its dimensions: The length across the top (outside length) is 11 feet, 5 inches, its height is 5 feet, 1 inch, the width is 9½ inches and its depth is 4½ inches.

The chimney has an ancient wooden hand carved hook pegged into the fireplace lintel butt. Individual stone steps descend to a dirt cellar on the south side of the chimney.

---

* The facing is plaster and its strong whiteness makes the front of the fireplace stand out boldly. Plastered fireplace fronts were much in evidence in the "old country". Illustrations of this are shown in *Old English Household Life,* by Gertrude Jekyll and Sydney R. Jones.

The parlor fireplace at the author's "Windmill Cottage" has a plastered face which is painted black.

Other illustrations in this volume show plastered fireplaces, for example, Courtland Manor at Tarrytown, N. Y., Mount Vernon (except for the lintel) and Salem Tavern in Old Salem, N. C.

108

NOAH WEBSTER HOUSE
West Hartford, Connecticut

This house was originally a rectangular structure of two rooms, one upstairs and one down, with an end chimney containing a large fireplace with two ovens in the back wall. The Captain Andrew Fuller House in Middleton, Massachusetts has a fireplace with two ovens in its back wall. While the presence of two ovens is not unique, it certainly is unusual.

The Noah Webster House merits attention, not only as a typical house of the early 1700's, but because it is the birthplace of an illustrious citizen of the early days, Noah Webster, Schoolmaster to America.

In 1963, the Webster House was designated a National Historic Landmark. It is now owned by the Noah Webster House Foundation.

At the left side of the fireplace, in front of one oven, a double or two back bars can be seen. No doubt they were often positioned over the fire to hold pots and kettles, in similar manner to a crane. In their present position, they would make a convenient shelf or stand for oven use.

The second oven on the right side does not show in the large picture. The entire hearth is composed of square, flat bricks. A very large brass kettle and a griddle hang from the lug pole.

Lovely molding and panelling surrounds the fireplace. The door is panelled and the over mantel space has four identical panels which together equal the width of the fireplace. The jambs and lintel are molded and fluted.

This close-up photo shows both of the two ovens.

Courtesy of Amos G. Avery

THE AVERY HOMESTEAD
Ledyard, Connecticut

The Avery Homestead, like the Fairbanks House in Dedham, has had a long line of Avery occupants. In fact the owner-occupant has been an Avery from 1757 to the present time. The house was built by William Morgan about 1696 as a four room structure with kitchen and parlor downstairs and two large chambers above.

Among the interesting features of the fireplaces in the house are an oven within the kitchen fireplace, a fireplace in the cellar, and an ash pit in the cellar for storage of wood ashes from which lye was obtained for use in making soap. The fireplace in the cellar may have been a slave's fireplace, or it may have been used for "par boiling" and as a scullery.

The kitchen fireplace room has exposed beams and the sheathing, paneled doors and over mantel are made of beautifully grained wood. The long fireplace crane supports a cauldron suspended by a peg and hole adjustable trammel. The oven door of sheet iron fits into an oblong opening in the back stone wall. The entire fireplace including the hearth is made of granite. The finely beveled mantel holds two early candlesticks, a pewter teapot and two hour glasses, while a double wick channel lamp or cruisie hangs from it. The old appurtenances in and around the fireplace include wrought iron andirons, an oven peel, foot warmer, toaster, waffle iron, warming pan, musket and a mortar and pestle.

THE GEORGE WYTHE HOUSE

Colonial Williamsburg, Williamsburg, Virginia

The home of George Wythe, the teacher of Jefferson, Marshall and Randolph. His name appears first among the Virginia signers of the Declaration of Independence.

The kitchen at the Wythe house, as in most Southern homes, is placed in a building apart from the main house. The principal reasons for so doing were to reduce the fire hazard and to avoid the heat of the fireplace in the main house. The smoke house too was an outbuilding instead of being tucked behind the chimney of the central fireplace.

Prepared food was carried by the servants from the kitchen to the house and accessories to keep it warm or to rewarm it in the house included plate warmers, trivets and pewter plates with hot water containers underneath.

The furnishings in this house are principally antiques of American "ancestry."

Of interest to note in the fireplace picture is the wooden rack on the chimney piece and the brick arch at the top of the storage space under the oven. Also a shelf is provided by means of an extended flat surface on top of the oven brick work. A wide assortment of fireplace furnishings are exhibited to include a number of copper and brass items. A coffee grinder rests on the table, coffee for which was roasted in the fireplace.

THE GOVERNOR'S PALACE
Colonial Williamsburg, Virginia

Rebuilt upon its original foundation which was excavated, the present structure succeeded the one ordered built in 1705. The house and gardens were considered to be the handsomest estate in Colonial America. Seven royal Governors and the first two Governors of the Commonwealth lived here. The Palace in Colonial Days was the scene of elegant social gatherings.

The furnishings throughout the Palace follow the English fashions of the time. They are all antique with the exception of several reproduction chandeliers.

The view of the fireplace shows a good part of the kitchen and shows us that earthenware bowls were used in food preparation and for holding food, and that pewter dishes were a mainstay in serving food. The fireplace has a brick arch instead of a lintel and the walls of the entire kitchen have been plastered. Instead of racks, boards with hooks are used for the purpose of hanging small utensils such as spatulas, ladles, forks and skimmers. Here too on the table is a coffee grinder, and a large cauldron hangs on a lug pole trammel.

OLD MANHATTAN KITCHEN
New York, New York

An interpretive replica of a Manhattan kitchen of three centuries ago is exhibited in the Museum of the City of New York. The Museum has successfully captured the flavor of the 17th century life in old New York when life was lived mainly in the kitchen. Mrs. Charlotte LaRue, associated with the museum, states that "although the main structure of the fireplace is a replica, the fireback and the tiles are genuine as are the objects and tools."

If for no other reason, this photograph is useful in showing a "cat", a very rare six pronged trivet, on which rests a kettle at the extreme right. Also shown are a spit rod and

Courtesy of Museum of the City of New York

a chain trammel, which holds a kettle tip and kettle. A rush light and candle holder combined is on the mantel. An "hour glass" is on the other end of the mantel.

One may question the valance or chimney cloth which is hung on the underside of the mantel, as a valid feature of the fireplace. However, Miss Margaret Stearns, Curator of Decorative Arts and Costume reports that:

> Chimney cloths may be seen in a great many Dutch paintings of the 17th century and are listed in numerous New York inventories. For example, the inventory of Margrita Van Varick 1695–6 lists two of flowered crimson gauze, one of green serge with fringe, and one painted chimie cloth.

In the book *"Old English Household Life"* by Gertrude Jekyll, two fireplace pictures show chimney cloths hanging from the mantel.

THE NEW ENGLAND KITCHEN
in the
HENRY FRANCIS duPONT
WINTERTHUR MUSEUM
Winterthur, Delaware

The kitchen, with its ample fireplace, is dated about 1740. It is based on the kitchen of a house in Oxford, Massachusetts.

The long granite lintel and the paneling on the wall around the fireplace are outstanding. A notable feature of the fireplace equipment is the clock spit or jack which by means of a weight and pulley causes the spit to rotate. The spit which is thus turned rests on spit hooks which are on the front of the andirons.

A drip pan for placement under roasting meat is shown on the hearth. Hanging on the wall at the right is a skewer holder and skewers and standing at the left is an oven peel. A brazier with a copper tea kettle resting on it are shown. Such a brazier is made with a flat pad at each corner for the purpose of receiving plates and vessels.

115

esy of the Henry Francis du Pont Winterthur Museum

KERSHNER KITCHEN
in the
HENRY FRANCIS duPONT WINTERTHUR MUSEUM
Winterthur, Delaware

It will be noted that the fireplace is built of stone. The farmhouse which contains the fireplace is dated about 1755 and came from Berks County, Pennsylvania.

The lintel, of white oak, is twelve feet long and the hearth is brick (original). An opening in the right back wall may seem to be a bake oven, but it is declared to be a fuel entrance into a "five plate stove" in a parlor on the other side of the wall.

Andirons are lacking in this fireplace; the fire logs are placed on the ashes. Skewers and a toaster hang from the lintel, and a waffle iron stands at the right jamb.

A lug pole up the chimney holds the trammel which in turn holds the hanging skillet.

A copper tea kettle rests on a long legged trivet, and several iron pots and pans are shown.

The small hanging cupboard on the right wall is a very fine primitive. The small drawers may have been used for spices.

116

I. E. LIVERANT HOUSE
Colchester, Connecticut

A very crude, primitive fireplace in the home of Mr. I. E. Liverant. It is in the cellar of the house which was built in 1761, being the third house on the site, the first one, a cabin having been built in 1699–1700.

The fireplace is referred to as a summer fireplace * and judging by the charred lintel, it has seen much use. There are two beehive ovens in the back wall of the fireplace, so

* Mrs. Henry W. Whitney reports on a cellar fireplace at "Whitehall", in Portsmouth, R. I. that "because of the pallets found there we know it was used by slaves."

much baking was done here, as well as par boiling, cooking and scullery work.

The Southern fireplaces in outbuildings had the advantage of removing a fire hazard as well as removing the heat of cooking from the living quarters.

The hand hewn oak lintel is approximately 11 feet long; the opening is 8½ feet long and 5 feet high. An unusual feature is the right jamb which is about twice as wide as the left jamb. The entire fireplace except for the lintel is made of field stone.

PARDEE-MORRIS HOUSE
East Haven, Connecticut

This fireplace, a huge one was constructed in the north stone wall of the 17th century house, a temporary one with bake oven, which was built after the British burned the old house. It has a stone sink on one side. Temporary though it was, the fireplace is still there.

from a report
by Mr. William L. Warren, Director
The Stowe-Day Foundation

The fireplace is more primitive looking than many of the early fireplaces. The huge oak lintel is roughly hewn with a broad axe and the stones have a rough surface. The rough stone bake oven is in the side wall and the fireplace itself, instead of being centered in the room, joins a corner of the room. There is no mantel above the lintel.

A diamond shaped candle sconce is attached to the over mantel and herbs hang from it above. A kettle hangs on a lug pole trammel. On the table by the fireplace one sees a chopping bowl, potato masher and a skimmer made of wood and an earthen slip-ware dish. Hanging from the lintel are pans, a ladle, a spatula and griddle.

118

Courtesy of Antiquarian and Landmarks Society of Connecticut; Photograph by Richard Gipstein

THE HEMPSTED HOUSE
New London, Connecticut

Built in 1678 by Joshua Hempsted, one of the founders of New London, and lived in continuously by Hempsted heirs until 1937, the House still stands on part of the original six acre grant Robert Hempsted received in 1645. It is one of the few 17th century houses in Connecticut and the oldest surviving house in New London. Some of the original family furniture and other possessions are still contained in the house. It is now owned and maintained by the Antiquarian and Land-marks Society of Connecticut. It has the original stone fireplace in the 17th century lean-to kitchen. The hearthstone is a single piece of granite.

Just as in the author's "retreat" home in New Hampshire, the herbs are hung on a wooden pole which is held by a series of hooks in the ceiling beams in front of the fireplace.

Some fine pewter chargers and a porringer are on the mantelpiece (a pewter coffee pot and an hour glass are out of sight). At the extreme right a hanging saucer candle holder is hooked to the lintel. If the picture were not taken from an angle, one would discover a rare heart-shaped skewer holder and a decoratively carved tobacco box which rests on a jamb shelf.

The fireplace and bake oven are built of stone and the sides of the fireplace are splayed. The lintel and overmantel are covered with a wooden sheathing. Several trammels hang from a lug pole, one of which holds a kettle.

On the hearth are an "Indian" mortar, a stool, toasting fork and a toaster, and a long legged skillet for cooking in coals or hot ashes. A small cast iron pot rests in the oven opening and hanging from the left jamb is a coal's carrier or pan. The housewife using this kitchen and fireplace must have been delighted to have a cupboard and shelves, which doubtless are made of pine. The crib in the foreground is a real primitive.

THE WENDELL DAVIS HOUSE

An "ancient" Connecticut fireplace with an ash well opening in the back wall. The ashes which were shovelled into this "hole in the wall", would fall into a cellar beehive ash pit for storage. The ash pit below was built into the central chimney.

Courtesy of Mr. Wendell Davis

BUTTOLPH-WILLIAMS HOUSE
Wethersfield, Connecticut

One of the finest examples of 17th century architecture in Connecticut is the Buttolph-Williams house at Wethersfield. All the furnishings are in keeping with the 17th century. In 1968 the Buttolph-Williams House was declared a Registered National Historic Landmark by the U. S. Department of the Interior. The building was found to "possess exceptional value in commemorating or illustrating the history of the United States."

A fine array of primitive wooden ware and fireplace hardware is shown in this fireplace. Also some very fine items of early lighting devices. On and over the mantel are two lanterns, the smaller a pierced tin lantern and the larger, one of the rarer and older lanthorns whose "windows" are made of horn. A tinder box and rushlight holder rest on the narrow mantel and a cruisie or grease lamp hangs above it.

A fine clock spit is in place, fixed to the mantel with the chains all ready to turn the spit bar which rests on the racks of the andiron columns.

Two huge lug pole, saw toothed trammels, hold kettles and an iron ring or hoop to hold pots and pans shows just below the lintel. Hanging at one side or the other are a spatula, a pot hook, a skewer holder and skewers, and at the right, an iron ladle. The andirons have what appear to be cresset finials which may be just a blacksmith's decoration. On the hearth are two peels, one wooden and one iron, a long handled frying pan, a toaster, two three-legged pans, a brass kettle and an adjustable toaster or roaster on a stand.

The house is maintained by the Antiquarian and Landmarks Society of Connecticut.

Courtesy of The Newton Bee *and Photographer R. Scudder Smith*

"THE OLD HOUSE"

Cutchogue, Long Island

The Old House at Cutchogue was built in 1649. As an example of 17th century domestic architecture of English origin, it is one of the most important early buildings in this country. The house was built at Southold, Long Island and moved shortly thereafter to Cutchogue.

The fireplaces are enormous—two of practically the same size: one in the living room and one in the kitchen. The kitchen fireplace, which is shown here, is nine feet five inches long, three feet deep and five feet high. A massive oak lintel supports the brickwork above the opening. There are supports in the throat of the chimney on which the lug pole rests. Pots and kettles are hung from the trammels which are "hooked" on the lug pole or trammel bar.

The fireplace in the sitting or "setting" room is unusual because of its size which matches the kitchen fireplace. Also its sides form a quarter circle and are constructed of curved brick. The same construction is seen in the Hart House fireplace at the Metropolitan Museum of New York which is illustrated among the fireplace pictures.

It should be noted that the brick oven in the kitchen fireplace has an arched opening which extends to the bottom on one side only. There are a goodly number of old cast iron pots and kettles exhibited which are in keeping with such an enormous fireplace. It is quite obvious that larger andirons and larger logs could be accommodated. That part of the hearth which extends into the room is constructed of square bricks.

Courtesy of Independent Congregational Church Society of Cutchogue

Courtesy of Sleepy Hollow Restorations, Tarrytown, New York

VAN COURTLANDT MANOR

on the Tappan Zee, Tarrytown, New York

The Ferry House kitchen is in the Van Courtlandt Manor—a Sleepy Hollow Restoration. Hearthside cooking demonstrations are a feature today. This fireplace is part of a late 18th century stone house. The Van Courtlandt family possessed the property from the 17th century until a few years ago—"one of the longest records of family occupation and ownership in the United States."

It will be noticed that the fireplace brick, in and out, has been plastered. Also there is much more brass and copper in use in this Dutch fireplace than in the early New England fireplaces. The kettles, tea pots, pans and ladles are of brass. There is a cast iron oven door which swings on hinges and certain other utensils are of iron, either cast or wrought. The cupboard near the fireplace has a fine display of pewter. Candles, in a lantern and in "hog scraper" type holders, furnish the light.

Courtesy of New Castle Historical Society

THE AMSTEL HOUSE

New Castle, Delaware

Built about 1730 for a Dr. John Ferney, the main portion probably incorporates parts of an older structure in its service wing. In Amstel House in 1794, President Washington attended the wedding of Ann Van Dyke to Kensey Johns, Sr. Nicholas Van Dyke, Sr. was an early governor. Amstel House now belongs to the New Castle Historical Society.

The kitchen and kitchen fireplace are equipped with utensils of the Colonial period. The pots, pans, skillets and kettles usual to this period are to be seen. In addition, a wooden candle box is hanging from the lintel at the left, and below on the hearth is an unusual plate warmer on legs. At the right is a settle over which are a pair of metal scales. On the long mantel are some fine examples of slip ware and two flintlock pistols; over the mantel a musket and a rifle are hung.

At the extreme top left and almost out of the picture a tin candle chandelier is hanging from the ceiling. One can see the wheel of a wool wheel and a crib on the floor.

DUTCH HOUSE
New Castle, Delaware

The line drawing is of the Dutch House in New Castle, Delaware, which dates from the mid-17th century. It is regarded as the oldest dwelling in the state. As a corner fireplace and with an arched lintel, it differs from most others in its shape. The andirons should be called fire dogs as they have the look. A spill holder is on the right hand jamb. The spinning wheel shown is an "unconventional" type similar to ones found in Canada. Two very early lamps hang from the mantel which is more in the nature of a shelf above the fireplace opening.

Courtesy of New Castle Historical Society

MOUNT VERNON

Mount Vernon, Virginia

Mount Vernon, the home of George Washington, has been restored and maintained by the Mount Vernon Ladies Association of the Union. This plantation house was built around 1743. During George Washington's occupancy with his wife, Martha Custis, the Mansion was enlarged and changed somewhat.

The kitchen fireplace, as was usual in the South, is in an outbuilding, and it has been equipped with utensils of the period. A few are authenticated as original, to include the crane, four or five pewter plates with hot water compartments, a trivet, an iron stand and a bell metal skillet. A large mortar in the scullery is also original. George Washington in his will bequeathed "the household and kitchen furniture of every sort and kind" to his wife Martha Washington.

A rack over the lintel holds four rods and a shelf on which are hung ladles, forks and skimmers. Many such implements also hang from the lintel itself. The pot hangers (except a trammel) have two arms which are joined at the top where they rest on the crane.* It is a typical Southern kitchen of a well-to-do family.

* This type of pot hanger which looks something like ice tongs is found solely in the South.

Courtesy of Old Salem, Inc.

SALEM TAVERN
IN OLD SALEM VILLAGE
Winston-Salem, North Carolina

A rare, if not unique, fireplace arrangement is shown in the Salem Tavern which was built in 1784 to replace a Tavern which burned that year.

Mr. Frank L. Horton of Old Salem, N.C. describes the adjoining fireplace as follows:

The left hearth is for scullery use with a bake oven opening through the back, the right hearth being the cooking area. These fireplaces are in our Salem Tavern Kitchen. The scullery and bakery function was removed to an outbuilding in 1815 and this fireplace closed. We reopened the oven opening and restored the fireplace arch in the 1950's.

The Southern kitchen fireplaces generally have a more orderly arrangement than in the North, for smaller utensils. Ladles, pans and other implements are hung on a bar with hooks, which is fastened to the wall. The rack between the fireplaces has a Southern style pot hanger which looks something like ice tongs. The clock jack is complete but the spit bar is against the wall instead of on the andiron columns where it rests when in operation.

Courtesy, Kenmore Association, Inc.

KENMORE

Fredericksburg, Virginia

A handsome Georgian Mansion of Col. Fielding Lewis, Patriot, and Betty Washington Lewis, only sister of George Washington, dates from 1752. It possesses some of the finest ceilings and overmantels in America.

This Southern outbuilding kitchen is used daily at the present time to make gingerbread and to heat hot water for tea. The gingerbread is made by the recipe of Washington's mother Mary.

A fine array of fireplace tools and utensils is shown in the picture of the fireplace. There are two cranes, one on either side, on which hang a goodly quota of kettles and pots. On the right hand side is a pair of unusual bellows, a salt box, an oven peel and several waffle irons. To the left of the brick oven is a warming pan with a turned wooden handle and on either side at the top of the lintel hang spoons and skimmers in wooden racks. The short andirons in the fireplace also have spit racks. A Dutch oven and skillet with short legs rest on the hearth. An excellent view is afforded of the rare wooden crane in the space of the overmantel, and herbs are hanging from it. A typical foot warmer is beside the cook's foot. Steelyards which are seen at only a few fireplaces are hanging from a nail or hook in the lintel.

Courtesy of Mr. Edward Durrel

THE DURELL FARM MUSEUM

at the Union Fork and Hoe Co., Columbus, Ohio

A replica of an Ohio home of the 1790–1820 era was erected as a Museum to house Mr. Durell's extensive collections. All of the building materials are early American. The very fine kitchen fireplace was dismantled in a house in the East and shipped to Columbus. It has two cranes, one on each side; each of which swings beyond the center of the fireplace. There is a narrow shelf or mantel over the lintel. The ceiling beams are exposed, and the floorboards are wide.

Wallace Nutting in his *Furniture Treasury* used an illustration of a fireplace in the home of L. P. Goulding of Sudbury, Massachusetts, and called it "The best furnished fireplace I know of." The Durell fireplace is included partly for the reason that it too is well furnished. A student of early American homes and fireplaces could learn a great deal about how our ancestors lived by examining the many implements which are exhibited here.

Fireplace Furniture:
The Tools and Utensils

FIREBACK

Philadelphia Museum of Art, Collection

This unusual fireback is made of cast iron
in three sections to fit the fireplace completely.
It is American, made in the 18th Century.

FIREPLACE FURNITURE:
THE UTENSILS AND TOOLS

Some of my readers may take me to task for showing or describing utensils which doubtless originated in England and were used principally in the old country. But so too did the settlers come from abroad and many of the implements came with them or were sent to the colonies on order. When the materials and workmen were available they were reproduced here. I heard an authority on lighting express doubt that rushes and rushlight holders were used in this country, and there may be those that will maintain that the use of the curfew or fire cover was not transferred to this country, because of their rarity. This conclusion does not take into account that they are rare in England, also.

One American writer on Colonial ways stated that the iron crane was a Yankee innovation about 100 years after the country was opened up and yet cranes were in use in England long before the Colonists reached these shores. The English books on Old Household Life and their Fireplace Implements illustrate very elaborate and ornate cranes and some with special devices to raise or lower the crane arm itself. Our ancestors not only brought with them some of the implements they were familiar with, but also they brought the experience, know-how, and craftsmanship to turn out products like those of their past home life.

Early Fireplace Equipment or "furniture" as Wallace Nutting called it, was quite essential to the use of the fireplace in its several capacities. For the purpose of description, the hardware which is indigenous to the fireplace will be called the *tools,* which are not to be confused with the kitchen fireplace accessories and utensils.

Nearly everyone who enjoys a fireplace at home, either for use or atmosphere, strives to acquire a few of the old implements whether the fireplace is an old or a new one. These may have been purchased at an antique shop or at an auction. A relatively few such items have "come down" in the family as the vast majority of implements have been disposed of by sale or as gifts to museums and historical societies.

The present owners, therefore, of the "decorative" fireplace utensils which are in private homes may know little about the origin of the items—as to whether they came from the old country or were manufactured or blacksmithed in the new country or where in America. Early fireplace equipment is much sought after and many pieces are becoming quite rare. There are quite a number of fireplace tools and utensils which are marked by the maker, and therefore, are identifiable to an extent by place and period, yet these are the exceptions.

The best manner in which to enumerate and describe the various furnishings for fireplace maintenance and use is to present a list with the names and description of each.

According to the author's designation the early fireplace tools are: lug pole, crane, wooden crane or hooks for drying purposes, andirons, poker, tongs, shovel, fork, trammels, pot hooks, bellows, fireback, fender, and back bar.

Fireplace Furniture: the Tools

A description of the fireplace tools, most of which are illustrated, follows:

Lug Pole or Trammel Stick: A thick green pole which is inserted in the throat of the chimney some six or eight feet high on which trammels and chain hooks were suspended. They in turn held pots and kettles as required.

Crane or Sway: In its simplest form the crane consists of a vertical and a horizontal bar of iron joined at right angles to each other. The vertical bar is the pivot, the ends of which are inserted in iron "eyes" which have been driven into the masonry one above the other. The distance between the eyes is determined by the length of the vertical bar of the crane.

The horizontal bar which swings out over the fire when in use is the suspension bar which is welded to the vertical or upright bar slightly below its top in order to be free of the upper eye.

A brace or cross bar is usually, but not always, joined diagonally between both iron bars for added strength.

Rather intricate cranes were made in England and came into only limited use in America, and mainly in Pennsylvania. Such cranes had an arrangement or device which would enable one to raise or lower the horizontal crane bar which gave the effect, though more limited, of an adjustable trammel.

The iron crane had a safety advantage over the lug pole which on occasion became charred through and let down its load. The crane also had the advantage of holding its load closer to the fire without such lengthy hooks and trammels as had to be used with a lug pole.

Andirons. The most widely known fireplace tools are the andirons. In supporting the wood while at the same time serving as a protective device, they run the gamut from small to large size and from plain to ornate. The metal used was mostly iron, both cast and wrought. When first used in the early kitchen fireplaces, andirons with a low front column were preferred or else they would be in the way when cooking or otherwise using the fireplace. Brass andirons which were imported in the early days were for chamber and parlor fireplace use mostly in "town" houses. Brass andirons became quite ornamental as well as practical.

When andiron spits, either of the skewer or bird cage variety, came into use, andirons needed sufficient height in their columns to carry racks or hangers to hold the spit bar. The racks were welded or cast onto the front or the backs of the columns. Two or more racks are often seen on old andirons so that the meat to be roasted could be held at different levels.

The andiron finials or tops were sometimes made in ring shape which enabled them to hold a spit bar without racks. Also the finials were occasionally in the form of cressets or "cup dogs" so that they could hold a mug or a candle or even a faggot. There are cresset andirons in the fireplace of Shakespeare's birthplace at Stratford-on-Avon in England.

Firedogs and andirons are synonymous terms. It so happened that certain stocky, short andirons gave the appearance of a dog, hence the name. However, any small andirons are sometimes referred to as firedogs.

Creepers are very small andirons which in some cases were put between large andirons for added protection from live coals falling forward. Upright prongs on the curved part or elbow of some andirons are called *Fender Posts* and serve in similar manner to creepers. Sometimes creepers were used solely as small andirons for a small fire.

Andirons not only served to control the fire by containing the logs, but they also allowed the fire to breathe. A good bed of ashes, however, underneath the andirons is useful to a good fireplace fire, nevertheless. The very first settlers of America were without andirons and of necessity the fireplace logs rested on a bed of ashes. There are several known andirons which have a swivel arrangement for changing the angle of the arm or log rest.

A *Drying Crane* made of wood is found over a few old fireplaces. This is fastened on the wall of the overmantel in such a way that it can be swung out in front of the fireplace. These cranes were used for the purpose of drying clothes, herbs, and certain fruits and vegetables—or in fact anything which needed drying before the fireplace. In some early houses one finds hooks which have been driven in the ceiling beams. In the author's summer retreat there are three parallel rows of hooks and one of the original poles remains which when placed in a set of hooks serves the same purpose as a wooden crane. The hooks, of course, are all in front of the fireplace where the best heat is obtainable.

Poker. This implement is said to have been little used. However, they are found in old inventories, and they generally accompany shovels and tongs. The poker has a dull point at its work end, and the handle end is sometimes shaped as a ring, perhaps for hanging on a hook or for a hand grip.

Tongs. A most useful instrument at a fireplace in the management of the fire. The common form of tongs has straight jaws flattened at the very bottom end in order to hold wood better, and an almost circular top end with the two tong rods working upon a hinge. The handle is generally squared with a knob or blunt spike at its end. They are made in various lengths ordinarily from 20 to 27 inches. The early ones were hand wrought by the local blacksmith, as were pokers, peels and other hand made implements.

Forks. Large fireplace forks for handling wood were very little in evidence and those which were, appear to be of a later period.

Fireback or *Fire Plate.* These were made of heavy cast iron and placed on the back fireplace wall principally to protect the brick or stone from the intense heat. The fireback also had the quality of reflecting heat and sending more of it out of the chimney place and into the room. Firebacks were cast in Pennsylvania, at Saugus, Massachusetts, and other locations, and invariably they had decorative designs and sometimes dates on them. There are "complete" firebacks by which I mean a three-sided fireback which will fit into the back wall and the two side walls of the fireplace (see illustration).

Trammels. There are long trammels and short trammels. The long ones were for use on the lug pole and the short ones for use on the crane. Also the trammels were of several types, e.g.

    a. Sawtooth or ratchet trammels. There are very few short ones. Most are long and were used with lug poles.

    b. Peg and hole trammels. These too were long and for lug pole use. There are a few short ones to go with cranes. They are sometimes called hook and eye trammels.

    c. Chain trammels. Almost exclusively a lug pole trammel. The chains have a hook on each end.

N. B. Philip Wright of England in his book on Old Farm Implements calls a trammel a "hake".

Pot Hooks or **Crane Hooks.** This type of holder was exclusively a crane hook. It was never long enough for lug pole use and was not adjustable. However, the author has a recently acquired pot hook which has three hooks welded on it which are several inches apart.

The pot hook was made in the shape of the letter "S" with a sufficient curve at the top and bottom to grab the crane at one end and a pot or kettle at the other end. This type of hook is reversible. As stated under trammels, there were several types and each type was made in short lengths for crane service but by no means as many as the longer ones to go with the lug pole. It is readily understandable why the crane hooks were shorter inasmuch as the crane is much nearer the fire than its predecessor the lug pole.

Back Bar. An iron rack with a bar supported by two uprights—one at each end of the bar. This bar was several feet high and was used with pot hooks to hang vessels over the fireplace in similar manner to the lug pole and the crane. However as in the case of the crane it could not swing from one position to another.

Bellows. This is a well known "tool" which serves to fan the embers or the blaze. A pair of bellows at the fireside has saved many a fire from going out and has saved the fire tender or maker much time by fanning embers until a blaze took hold of the wood. The author has in his collection a rare double bellows which has its nozzle in the middle of one side and can be pumped at either end, or both ends, alternately.

Shovel. A tool which was rarely absent from the fireplace, but which was useful primarily for shifting embers or handling ashes.

Idleback. A contraption which had its beginning in England and was introduced in America but relatively little used and, therefore, scarce in this country as far as can be determined. In effect the idleback or the tilter as it was sometimes called was a very practical device which enabled a tea kettle to be tipped and poured while still on the crane provided that the kettle's handle was affixed parallel to its snout. The tipper hung on the crane and had two claws with which to hold a kettle's handle. The kettle was then tipped by a little downward push at the end of a rod or arm of the idleback which extended out of the fireplace opening.

Fender. The wide and broad hearth of the early fireplaces made the fender less indispensable and yet when obtainable in some form they served well by containing ashes which might have spilled out and caused trouble. A section of an old wagon wheel rim, which might be four inches in width, has been known to be pressed into use as a fender.

Oven peel. The peel, sometimes called a slice is a thin, flat, long-handled shovel for use in putting bread, pies, etc. into or taking them out of the hot brick oven. A few peels were made of wood, but wrought iron peels were much more commonly used.

Utensils

The above are the tools and equipment of the fireplace. The tools were used in its operation and maintenance. In this regard they differ from the utensils which are used in and about the fireplace, but not for its maintenance.

Utensils, furnishings, hardware, implements and accessories are all words which have been used and have meaning in describing the assortment of vessels and appurtenances that have a place in the kitchen for fireplace use. It would be quite proper to call many of the "furnishings" kitchenware, but this author prefers to call them fireplace utensils and in so doing include not all kitchen implements, but only those which have a direct or indirect association with the fireplace. Then there is an additional category of related items which are associated with the kitchen fireplace because it was the center of activity and radiated warmth and cheer. This last group includes the butter churn, the spinning wheel, the cheese press, the candle molds, the musket or flintlock gun, the pipe and tobacco box, and the dye pot.

The fireplace tools and utensils are almost all illustrated and described separately, and they are identified also in the photographs of the fireplaces themselves. It is repetitious, in a sense therefore, to list and describe them here but such repetition may serve a good purpose by impressing the reader with the number and variety of the utensils and their uses in cooking and in the housewife's chores to which the fireplace contributed a share.

A list of utensils—their names and an alternate name if there is one and a brief description—follows:

Pipe tongs or *brand tongs* or *ember tongs.* Used to hold embers with which to light pipes. Usually have a pipe bowl reamer or cleaner attached and a flat tamper built in.

Warming Pan. To hold live coals for use in warming the bed.

Foot Warmer. A tin box in which hot coals are placed to warm feet especially when in sleigh, buggy or at church, in cold weather.

Fire Carrier or *Ember Shovel.* To carry coals from place to place. Small holes in the bottom gave air and some had a sliding cover.

Spit. Used to hold meat when roasting. *Skewers* pinned the meat in place. Some spit bars were made with a basket or cradle built in at the middle of the bar which could hold the roast without the use of skewers. Also some spit bars had horizontal iron spikes or prongs attached which would pierce and hold a roast in place.

Trivet or *Rest.* Small iron or brass stand with three legs on which to rest kettles or pots or other things. Related to the trivet is a plate *rest* which has two hooks at one end to go over a crane or fender. This has a handle like the ordinary trivet and the plate rest part in some will slide in and out.

Waffle Iron. For making waffles. More numerous than the wafer iron as it was used much more frequently.

Wafer Iron. For making wafers, thinner and fancier than waffles, used especially for holiday or church wafers.

Grisset or *Grease Pan.* To hold grease or tallow liquid for the dipping of rushes.

Skillets or *Frying Pans.* In a variety of sizes and some with quite long handles.

Pans. Of different sorts and sizes, some for hanging on the crane and some for standing in the ashes.

Toasters. Long handled with a swivel device for turning, also a shorter handled 3 legged kind, the toast holder of which will rotate on a pivot. There is also a standing toaster with prongs which slide up and down.

Griddle or **Gridiron.** For broiling. Now and then one finds a grooved griddle for running the meat juices into a built in cup.

Bird wings. For sweeping the hearth or table.

Salamander. A thick, short handled peel—when heated—used to brown bread loaves or cake baked in the brick oven. Oak leaves were often put under loaves to keep their bottoms clean.

Tea kettles. One type with a flat prong in front for tipping when the handle is at a right angle to the snout. The other type has the handle parallel to the snout and is the kind for which the idleback was designed.

Potato rake. A small curved piece of iron with a wooden handle to rake potatoes from the ashes.

Game Spit. See spit.

Footman. Similar to a trivet but with four legs. Has the same purpose in serving as a rest for kettle, plate or pan. Some have a brass top, the front of which is filigreed or pierced.

Skewers and **skewer holders.** The skewers are iron pins which pierce a roast and go through slots in the spit bar and thus hold the roast and enable it to be turned while cooking. The skewers are hung on a skewer holder when not in use. The tin kitchen or roasting oven also has a small turnable spit bar with slots for skewers.

Pots and **Pans.** There is an assortment of sizes in the pots and pans. Some of the pots have only three short legs for use in the coals or ashes and a handle for hanging on a crane. Pans ordinarily have no hanging handle but rather a horizontal handle for hand use and the legs are fairly long as compared with those of pots and kettles.

Smoke Jack. Seldom used but its purpose was to have the gases and smoke emerging from the chimney turn vanes which by means of a chain turned the spit in front of the fireplace. There is one in the chimney of the Wentworth-Gardener House in Portsmouth, N. H. and the author has heard of no other which has survived.

Bottle Jack. A jack which has a key to wind a spring inside the jack, will, when wound up, rotate a disc or wheel which has hooks hanging from it. Such a jack is made of brass and is made to hang from a holder attached to the mantel.

Clock Spit Jack. A more intricate and earlier jack was fastened to the lintel or the wall of the overmantel and as it unwound it turned a spit rod on the andirons by means of a chain. The clock spits are supposed to have been in use long before the tin reflector oven came into use.

Earthenware Pot. Cakes and small loaves were baked under a redware pot turned upside down in the ashes.

Tinder Box. A tin or brass, usually round, box of small size and with a lid on which a candle holder has usually, but not always, been affixed. Inside the box is a flint and steel and tinder with a tin cover over the latter. Sparks were obtained to light the tinder by striking the flint with the steel. The author has an oblong wooden box which looks like a knife box, but hangs up and has firemaking material in it.

Kettles. Of large or small size. Sides of a kettle extend outward from bottom to top whereas a cauldron has a wider belly or larger circumference at its middle, after which and before which it narrows or slants inward.

Cauldron. See explanation under kettle. Large brass cauldrons were used to heat milk in cheese making, among other uses.

Ladles, Skimmers, **and** *Strainers* were in daily use for just what their name implies. They were kept on racks by the fireplace or hung on nails and hooks. They had to be handy to the fireplace.

Bean Pot. This utensil is much the same the country over and in generation after generation. It is made of baked clay known as pottery, or earthenware.

Lid Lifter. A small hook with a wooden handle used to lift the lid of a pot or kettle for inspection or when the contents are ready to serve.

Candleholders of the socket type were used around the fireplace. These often had a long arm to hang on the lintel or mantel and reach down near or in front of the fire. Candles were hard to come by and expensive for a time. They served to supplement the light of the fireplace.

Pipe Rack. A pipe holder for the long clay pipes which when cleaned were placed before the fire in the racks to dry.

Pipkin. Stoneware or any kind of earthenware with handles and a lip and made with a dull glaze. They were used either seated in the ashes or raised on trivets.

Coffee Roaster. A cylindrical container for coffee which has a long handle and can be shaken or turned when over the fire.

Potato Basket. A round wire basket or cage with a wire handle which, with potatoes in it, could be immersed in boiling water and taken out when the potatoes were cooked, as a single load.

Spatula. A small flat shovel type implement with a relatively short handle used to turn griddle cooked food. Looks like a miniature peel.

Candle Box. A cylindrical or oblong box usually of tin but sometimes brass in which candles are kept. Most boxes have two straps with holes punched in them so they can be hung on nails or hooks near the fireplace.

Bannock Board. Made of wood and positioned when in use in front of the fireplace on the hearth. Cakes of corn meal were cooked on such a board.

Embercan. A can to stow ashes in when removed from the oven, if no storage space was available in the brick work.

Spice or *Coffee Mill.* A simple mill was attached to the wall before the box-like type for table use was introduced. The wall mill has a cup placed under the grinder and the box mill has a small drawer to catch the ground coffee or spice.

Goffering Iron. A useful iron for women in "primping". This iron when heated was inserted in a sheath or tube-like receptacle which is on a small stand. The hot tube was then used for ironing ruffles (crimping or fluting) by drawing them over it. The goffering iron is not to be confused with the toddy iron which is larger and longer.

Drip Pan. Such a pan is placed under the roast on the spit in order to catch the fat and juices of the meat as it cooks. An occasional griddle has a built-in drip pan.

Toddy Stick or *Iron.* An iron rod with a head on it something like a soldering iron. When heated red hot it was plunged into the toddy. A toddy stick is never rounded at the end like a goffering iron. Another name for it is "loggerhead".

Chestnut Roaster. Something like a miniature warming pan but has a flat rather than a rounded bottom. It is made of brass, and the cover is usually decorated.

Spills or *Lighters.* Strips of paper rolled into a stiff tube, the ends of which are pinched lightly to keep them from unwinding. The spills are often kept in a paper cornucopia or a box near the fireplace and used to light candles after the spill itself is lighted in the fireplace.

Hearth Brush. A bird's wing or shredded bark tied to a pole or stick at its lower end. See also under "bird's wings".

Iron Roaster or *Toaster.* A three-legged vertical shaft on which there is a sliding device which has spikes or hooks on it. The height can be set at different levels.

Brazier. A small "stove" in which charcoal or coals are placed. It looks like a kettle but has an opening in the side for draft and a grid top on which to heat or cook food.

Tin Kitchen or *Roasting Oven.* In several sizes; used to roast or bake before the fire.

Dutch Oven. A heavy iron pot with a heavy cover. The cover has a rim which holds live coals when placed on the cover to get a more even heat for baking.

Oven Light. A tin whale oil lamp with long wooden handle used to check status of food in the oven. Used after whale oil became available—around 1800 and after.

Most of the utensils were made of wrought or cast iron; little wood was used, mostly in handles, also frames for foot warmers, a few oven peels and an oven door occasionally. Copper and brass were utilized in kettles, ladles, skimmers, strainers and warming pans. Occasionally one would find a vessel made of bell metal. Pottery vessels were limited chiefly to the bean pot, pipkin, dyepot and a few other earthen pots.

There is still another group of household implements which cannot be called, properly, fireplace utensils but which do have a place here because of their association or relationship to the fireplace. I refer to the spinning wheel, the butter churn, the cheese press, the dye pot, the musket or flintlock gun with its powder horn, candle making implements, tobacco boxes and pipes. Most, if not all, of these implements will be seen in one or more of the fireplace illustrations.

One finds references, in early correspondence and in inventories, to fireplace utensils and an example of each follows:

In 1645, a correspondent named Mrs. Lake, sent to England a list of things she desired for the furnishings of a new house for her daughter. Among other things she asked for:

> a peare of brass andirons
> a brass kittel
> a warming pan
> a big iron pott
> a small stew pan of copper
> a drippe pan
> a skillet
> a pestel and mortar.

There were certain fireplace utensils and tools which were predominately used or even confined in their use to the town houses or the houses of the well to do. Several of these have been listed among the utensils already, as for example the fireback or fireplate, creepers and brass trivets. In addition there is the—

Invalid's charcoal stove. A square sheet iron receptacle for fuel. Each top corner has a flat pad the purpose of which is to hold plates for warming or kettles for heating.

Plate Warmer. Brass or sheet iron or even tin container, usually in the shape of a cylinder on legs. An open front is wide enough to insert plates one on top of the other. It looks much like a hood. One is shown in the fireplace photo in the home of Mrs. William Roelker. One type also consists of a series of vertical prongs on a stand within which plates are set.

Cat. A very rare six pronged plate or pot holder. It is a type of trivet with three prongs as legs and three prongs on the top side to hold the plates or dishes. One is shown in the exhibition fireplace photo of an old Manhattan fireplace at the Museum of the City of New York.

Curfew, or Fire Cover. A brass hood with or without air vents which was placed over the embers to contain them during the night but yet to keep them "alive". The curfew as we know it today was derived from the use of this device which for a period of time in England and the colonies was prescribed by "law" and a time of night set for its use. The brass curfew has almost disappeared. The only ones known by the author are in the Victoria and Albert Museum in London and the Brighton Museum in Brighton, England. Mrs. Josephine Peirce wrote that "First a fire was buried, preserved in the ashes of the fire itself. Later when man worked with metals the curfew or fire cover was invented."

Fire Screen. A wooden floor stand on which a cloth in a frame could be raised or lowered to protect one's face or body from the heat. There were a few small screens also for table use. See Fire Fan.

Comfortier. A little brazier of metal in which small coals could be handed about for pipe lighting.

Fire Fan. Looks like a hand fan which was used to screen the face from the heat of the fireplace. A small table screen served in the same manner, and the floor screen shielded the body. See Fire Screen.

Smoothing or Sad Iron, Iron Trivets and Tailors Goose. The author is at a loss to know when the first flat (sad) irons came into use, but among the earliest is a container with an ironing bottom which holds an iron slab. After the slab or block of iron is heated adequately, it is inserted in the holder, to provide heat for the iron. Special trivets were made to fit the flat iron, and the earliest were wrought iron. The tailors "goose" is a long and heavy flat iron, the handle of which is joined to the iron at the front end only in some and at both ends in others.

The ancestral housewife was adept at using her limited supply of pots and kettles which came over with the first settlers, from the "old country". As more settlers or colonists arrived, iron foundries were established and blacksmiths plied their trade. Fireplace utensils multiplied, for by 1840 more than 200 of these were advertised.

An Inventory of 1663 which illustrates the importance attached to the fireplace utensils in those days. The utensils constitute a major part of this inventory. The furniture is lumped together whereas the fireplace equipment is listed separately, in most instances.

Warwick this 11th d August 1663
An Inventory of ye goodes and Chattells of Mr. John Smith deputey of Warwick Late discessed

	£ s d
Inprimis in Plate one beaker one solt halfe of dozen of Spones	04–10–00
2 feather beds and furniture	10–00–00
2 diaper Tabell Cloathes and a dozen natkines	01–10–00
16 pieces of peweter	03–00–00
2 Brasse Candell Stickes a morter and pestle	00–10–00
1 Great Ketle	01–10–00
2 Smaller Ketles	00–10–00
1 bras Skillet	00–05–00
1 Iron Ketell one gun with poweder and shott	01–10–00
2 brasse pans Litell ones	00–10–00
1 spit	00–02–00
2 payer of Andieres fire shovell and tonges	00–10–00

1 payer of pott hangers 1 payer of pott hookes 00–06–08

A Cubord one round table and 4 Joine Stooles 00–10–00

2 Chaires 00–05–00

—The Early Records of the Town of Warwick, R. I.

In the next century we find many advertisements in the *Boston Gazette* and the *Boston News Letter* which list fireplace utensils for sale at "vendues." Some of the gleanings from these newspapers which refer to such items follow:

Pewter and Brass ware to be sold by Gilbert and Lewis Deblois at the sign of the Crown and Comb on Queen St., a large assortment of Brass Kettles, Skillets, Tea Kettles, Warming Pans, etc.

Boston Gazette, September 17, 1751.

Mr. Nathaniel Austin, Pewterer, makes and sells as cheap for cash or Old Pewter, as any person in Boston, the following articles . . . . He also has to dispose of at a reasonable rate, a small assortment of Braziers ware, viz Iron pots and kettles, shovel and tongs, Brass kettles, Warming pans, skillets, Frying pans, Tea kettles, Candlesticks, best London glue, Bellows.

Boston Gazette, October 3, 1763.

Braziers Wares—Mary Jackson at the Brazen-Head in Cornhill makes and sells . . . Hearths, Fenders, Shovels and Tongs, handirons, candlesticks.

Boston Gazette, September 27, 1736.

Braziers Shop—Thomas Russell, Brazier, near the Draw-bridge in Boston, makes, mends and new-tins all sorts of Braziers wares viz Kettles, Skillets, frying pans, Kettle pots, sauce pans, tea kettles, Warming pans, Wash basins, skimmers, ladles, etc.

Boston News Letter, October 30, 1740.

Cutlery and Tools—Just imported by Edward Blanchard and to be sold at his shop on Union St. 'Cheap for cash' . . . Brass kettles, skillet and warming pans, brass and iron candlesticks, . . . steel brass and brass head dogs, steel brass and iron head tongs and shovels, bellows of all sizes, neat chamber bellows with brass noses, large and small fire pans, tea-kettles . . . iron ladles, hearth brushes.

Boston News Letter, July 17, 1760.

Kitchenware—Imported from Bristol & London by William Jackson and sold at his shop at Brazen Head, a great variety of articles, including chafing dishes, box and flat irons, roasting jacks.

Boston Gazette, September 27, 1764.

Mary Jackson and Son—having opened their shop since the late fire, a few doors from the Courthouse where customers may be supplied with . . . Brass kettles, skillets, warming pans, frying pans, iron pots, kettles and skillets . . . andirons, shovels and tongs, fire pans, brass and iron candlesticks . . . japan'd snuffers.

The upper two tea kettles, one of which is on a trivet, have their handles parallel to the snout and thus must be lifted by a person in order to pour. The two lower tea kettles both have a "tipper" attached to the upper front part which can be pressed down for pouring while still on the crane. It will be noticed that these kettles differ from the later stove kettles by having "nubbin" legs to help them settle more evenly into ashes, for one thing.

Also shown in the picture, at the bottom left is a small pan on a trivet, above which is an idleback or tipper—a device to hold at the top the type of kettle which has its handle parallel to the snout. The idleback has a long arm, and with a little pressure on its tip end it will cause the kettle to be tilted for pouring without lifting it from the crane. In one of the fireplace photographs the idleback will be seen holding a kettle from the crane and with its arm projecting outward.

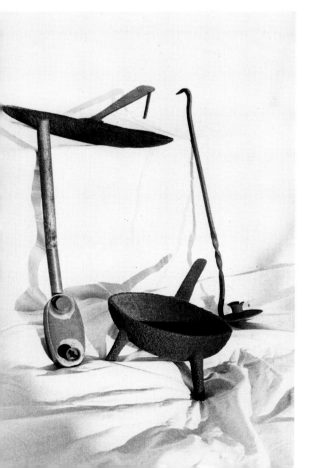

This illustration has to do with light in and around the fireplace. A saucer candleholder fastened to a long arm can be hung on a hook or the mantel, to supplement the firelight when cooking. The oval tin whale oil lamp with a long wooden handle was used as an "oven light" to look at the bread or cake in the bake oven. The two middle objects are rare grissets in which rushes are soaked or dipped in fat or tallow to make the rushlight. Grissets when in use are placed near the fire to keep the fat liquefied.

143

Foot warmers, four in number and of different sizes, are shown. The very top one is oval in shape. Except for the flattish tin one which could be a bed warmer as well as a foot warmer, each one is perforated tin in a wooden frame. A tin door is the opening for the insertion of a tin tray or pan which when used contains coals of fire for use in buggy or sleigh or in the unheated church of that day. The foot warmers which travel are supplied with a wire handle.

The middle box warmer has nicely turned corner posts and is the type and size commonly used. The flat tin warmer is made to use hot water instead of coals.

The real Dutch oven is pictured here. It is a cast iron pot with a cast iron cover. It can be set in the coals and ashes on its three legs or it can be hung from the crane by its handle of wrought iron. The cover, which has a lifting handle, also has a rim fully around its circumference. This helps to contain live coals which are spread on the cover when baking corn pone or other food in the fire. The brick oven is often erroneously called a Dutch oven. The lower photo shows the Dutch oven with its cover off.

144

A selection of griddles for broiling meat in the coals. All are on legs which are set in the coals and ashes. The round griddles, which Wallace Nutting called swirling griddles, can be rotated—while the handle and legs remain stationary. The griddle at the far right is of a later date than the others, and it is enameled and grooved to catch the meat juices.

A bottle jack is shown on its side, below which is a ring with hooks on it. This is attached underneath the jack and revolves slowly as a spring in the jack unwinds. The hole in the jack is where the winding key is inserted. When the jack is hung before the fire, game, such as rabbits or partridge, is made to turn and roast more evenly by this mechanical device.

The three-legged implement pictured is a toaster or a roaster depending upon the purpose for which it is used. There are four two-pronged "spikes" on which game, toast or whatever can be placed. The iron ring around which the spikes are fixed can be raised or lowered to the desired height when placed before the fire.

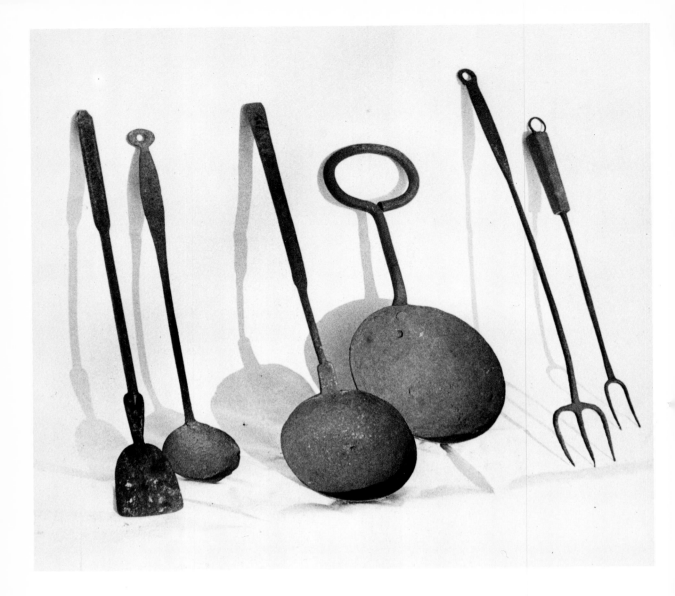

A grouping of forks, ladles and a spatula. The two smaller ladles were probably used in cooking, but the short handled large ladle may have been used for heavier work such as in soap making or preparing tallow for candlemaking. Two of the utensils have a rolled end as a lip for hanging, while the others have a ring or eye.

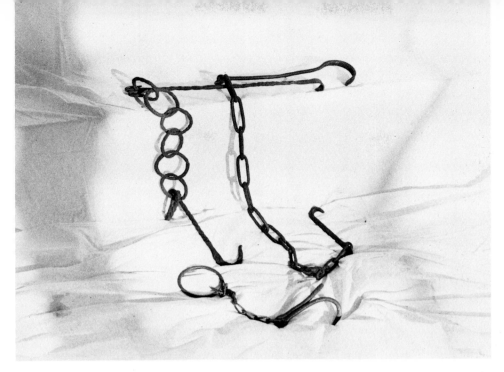

Two lug pole chain trammels. The end with the larger hook goes over the lug pole. The end with the smaller hook receives the pots and kettles. Below the chain trammels is a crane hook. The ring goes over the crane bar or a pot hook. The anchor type hooks are to hold meat.

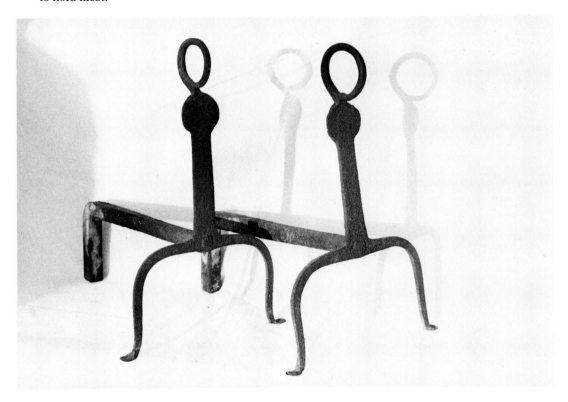

Typical early andirons of wrought iron. The top rings are useful to hold a roasting or drying bar, and they are also ornamental. The artisan blacksmith made the legs graceful as well as practical.

Two pipe racks or holders in which the long clay pipes were put to dry after cleaning. These were placed on the hearth before the fire. The "gadget" which is lying flat is a pipe tong. It is used to take embers for lighting pipes out of the fire.

An assortment of waffle irons. The handles serve to open and close the irons as well as to hold them by. A clasp at the end of the handles enables them to be locked so they may be put in the hot ashes or fire without holding them together by hand

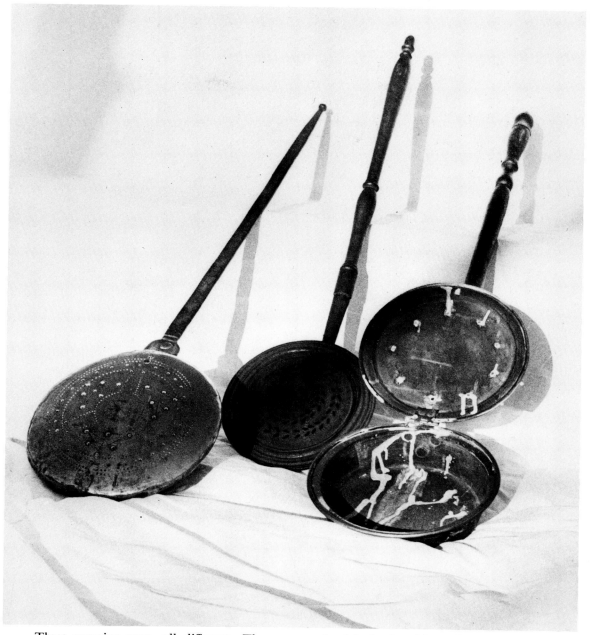

Three warming pans—all different The one on the left is the oldest; the pan is copper and the handle wrought iron. The center warming pan is made of sheet iron and is very rare. The handle is wood. The one which is open is made of brass with a wooden handle and might be called the conventional type.

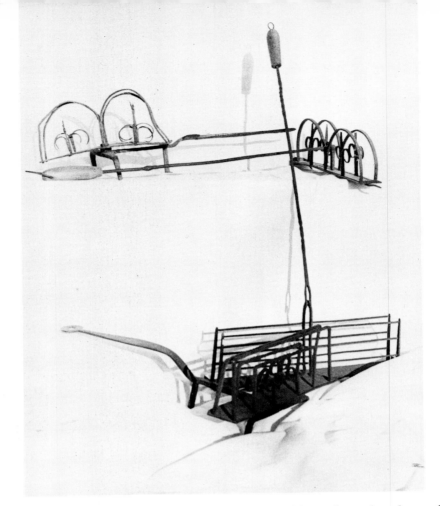

An assembly of toasters. At the top level is a toaster which stands on three legs and can be put into the hot ashes. The part which holds the material to be toasted is made to turn on a pivot; the other longer handled toaster has a swivel and will turn at a flip of the wrist.

The two toasters "jumbled" together below also illustrate each type of toaster. The swivelled long-handled type is very plain and practical in appearance whereas the smithy has shown his skill and imagination in making the other one and the two above.

A group of skillets for fireplace use. The long handled ones allow a person to stand further away from the heat of the fire. The hooks at the end of the handle make it possible to hang the skillets on a hook or nail when not in use. In these early skillets the handles are riveted to the pans!

The wife of an early settler had to select her own size to suit, or make do with one size only. On occasion a large kettle or cauldron was passed around from one house to another.

These three cauldrons are typical cast iron vessels which served many purposes. There was always a kettle of hot water on the fire. Kettles were used for cooking many kinds of food. Each of these has its own wrought iron handle and its three rather short legs. They could hang over the fire from a crane or the more primitive lug pole or sit in the fire for greater heat. Today some are used for atmosphere and some for outdoor flower pots, but they are hard to obtain.

A set of 3 cast iron skillets with legs of medium length are nestled together. This type of vessel had a great deal of use in fireplace cookery. This applies also to the two wrought iron pans, one of which has its legs almost "burned" through from sitting in the fireplace coals.

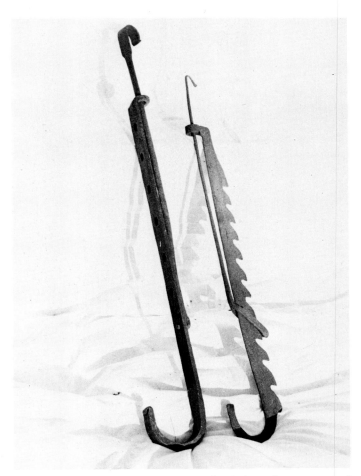

One sawtooth or ratchet trammel on the right and a hole and peg trammel on the left. Each is designed to accomplish an adjustment of the height of whatever is hung on it. The end with the larger hook goes around the lug pole, while the hook on the end of the adjustable rod is to hold the pots and kettles. In other words the trammels are upside down, but they stood up better for a picture this way.

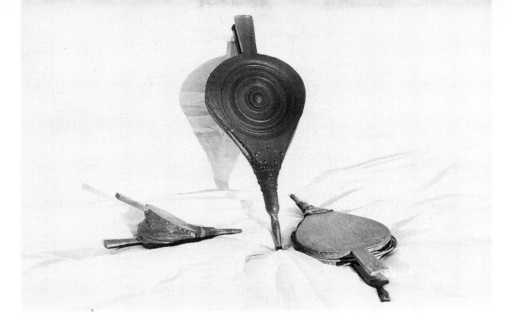

Three pair of bellows, of different sizes, but all for the fireplace. They are extremely useful in starting a fire or fanning a blaze from embers by feeding oxygen to the fire. The bellows have nozzles of iron or brass. They are constructed of leather between a back and front of wood. Handles aid in compressing and expelling the air which enters by a vent in the back side.

The small tin at the top was used for baking apples or potatoes or roasting small game. The larger roasting or reflector ovens are called tin kitchens. They are even referred to as Dutch ovens, although incorrectly. The open part which shows here is intended to face the fire. A front door which can be made to swing open enables the cook to inspect or to baste the roast without getting between the oven and the fire, or turning it around. A spit runs through the center of the oven in which rod there are slits or holes to accommodate the skewers when attaching a roast. There is a circle of holes punched in the side of the oven where the spit enters and a prong on the handle can be inserted in any one of the holes which will hold the spit in a certain position. By changing the prong from hole to hole the spit and roast can be rotated.

The bottom row from left to right includes an oven peel made of sheet iron with a long wooden handle. This was acquired in the South and is often called a slice. The next all-iron long-handled peel is a more common variety, especially in the North, as is the fourth in this row. Between the two wrought iron peels is a wooden spatula, which also could be used to take a pie or bread from the oven. The holes in one end of this device make a perfect hand grip. It should be noticed how the blacksmith expressed his individuality and artistry in shaping the finial or handle end of the iron peels.

Another wooden spatula or peel behind the larger iron peel is almost oval in shape and delicate in thickness and size. A long handled wooden peel lies horizontally in the background. All of the peels have thin edges at the bottom end so that they will slide under a loaf of bread or a pie.

154

CURFEW OR FIRE COVER

This curfew is in the Smithsonian Institution in Washington, D. C. It is made of sheet brass, is conical in shape and is chased and perforated with simple but ornamental designs. A curved handle is attached to the edge of the curfew. The curfews were used probably in well-to-do homes exclusively and are now extremely rare. The only other one which the author knows about is in the Victoria and Albert Museum in London.

The curfew was used to cover live coals for the night much as ashes were commonly used to cover the embers in the absence of a curfew.

The use of a curfew served a double purpose, reducing or entirely avoiding the hazard of a house fire while at the same time keeping alive some embers with which to start the hearth fire anew the next morning.

A brass curfew or fire cover, which the author discovered and purchased recently—a very rare article.

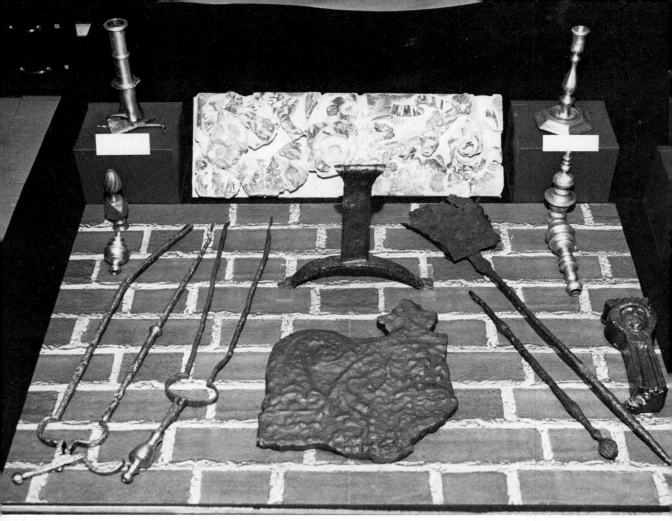

Courtesy of Colonial Williamsburg

ARTIFACTS OF THE EARLY FIREPLACE

In the archaeological collections at Colonial Williamsburg, there are numerous items of fireplace equipment. These artifacts were brought to light as a result of excavations, preliminary to the restoration of that pre-Revolutionary Capital.

The items, shown in this photograph, include a fireback fragment, part of andirons and brass andiron finials, tongs, a poker and a shovel or peel. This arrangement and photograph were provided through the courtesy of Mr. I. Noël Hume, Director of the Department of Archaeology.

If evidence were needed to confirm the type of tools which were used in the Colonial fireplace, these artifacts and their source are sufficient verification.

A "Pennsylvania" candle drier which holds a number of individual round dipping devices. These are removed from a hook on the end of the arms when used for dipping candles and returned when the candles are fully dipped and ready for drying.

A kettle tip or idleback suspended by a hook from a crane. It in turn supports a kettle which it can cause to pour. A long arm which extends out of the fireplace is pressed downward for this operation.

A cast iron pudding or cake mold and an unusual kettle. A cast iron handle for pouring extends half way across the top of the kettle, which has a pouring snout.

A rare combination is shown in this picture: an early fireback of cast iron; a wrought iron crane hook with three racks or hangers; and a brass plate rest.

157

Pipe holders for drying clay pipes before the fire.

Pipe tongs for removing embers from the fire to light pipes, and pipe and tobacco box with single pipe.

Smoothing irons and iron trivets, with "tailor's goose" in background.

A variety of trivets, the two middle ones of brass, and the one on the left of iron. At the extreme right is a plate rest made to fit on a fender.

Fireplace trivet with sliding (adjustable) rests for handle of ladle in pot or kettle.

Round wafer iron showing the pattern or design.

Oblong wafer iron showing the design.

All warming pans: Left to right, copper pan with wrought iron handle, brass pan with wooden handle and a rare sheet iron pan with wooden handle.

Two long-handled skillets or frying pans, which are becoming quite scarce.

Left to right: A sheet iron "slice" (southern style), a waffle iron, and a long-handled toaster or broiler.

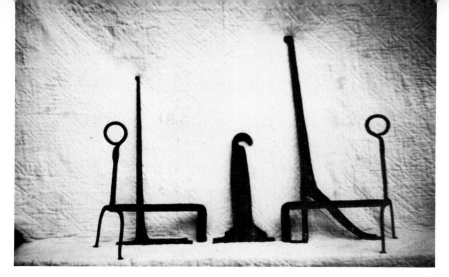

A pair of hand wrought andirons with ring at top of column to hold a spit bar. The two cranes standing on end are somewhat different from the usual. The one on the left has no diagonal support bar, and the one on the right does not have the full vertical or upright bar. The middle crane is not for fireplace use but is made to hold large steelyards.

Two grissets, one with stubby legs, the other with a handle leg only.

Two crane meat hooks, a cast iron kettle, and a large cauldron ladle.

Bellows for the fireplace, used to fan the embers in starting or livening the fire.

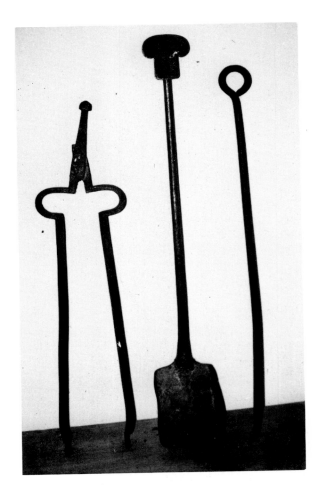

A fireplace tongs, oven peel and poker.

Left to right: A solid flat griddle; a flat-bottom pan with heavy fixed bail, and a hanging ring for a pot rest. Each bail or arm has a ring for use in hanging on a crane.

This illustration shows the hanging ring in action holding a pan which, however, could be hung by itself. The other utensil is a trivet with a ring top, which holds a pan with a rounded bottom.

Left to right: A three-legged kettle or pan, whose bail has a ring in its middle for use on a crane; a doughnut kettle or, according to Wallace Nutting, a rare original double boiler, and a long-handled spider on legs.

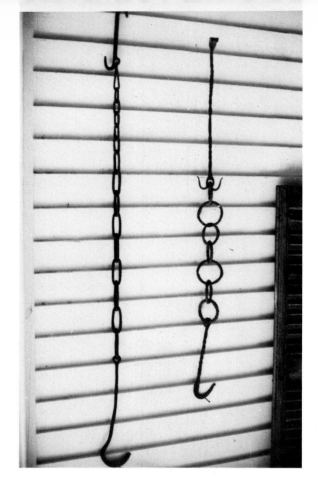

A couple of chain lug pole trammels.

A sawtooth or ratchet trammel is between two peg and hole trammels. These are adjustable types of pot hooks.

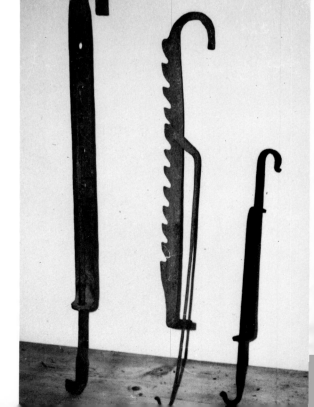

Two cast iron kettles, one of which has its own tipper. The other needs to be removed from the crane in order to pour, or else one must use a kettle tip or tilter, which is shown in the center.

Cast iron pots or cauldrons which have short legs and handles, for use on or over the fire.

The real Dutch ovens, the covers of which have rims to contain coals, which are placed on them to obtain a more even heat.

Braziers for burning charcoal or other fuel. The one on its side shows the heart design in its grill.

An assortment of pot holders. The one on the extreme right is built something like ice tongs and is found chiefly in the South.

A pot lid lifter on each end, two gophering-irons and a toddy-heating receptacle, which is stuck in the coals or hot ashes.

A charcoal or invalid's stove. Pads at corners are for plate rest. The lanthorn, with horn windows, is at the right.

A group of brass kettles. Shown with the largest one is a wooden dasher with which to stir apple butter.

The same brass kettles, but with the dasher in place. The horizontal bar fits on the kettle's handle. The hand crank, shown better in the top photo, operates the dasher.

These three griddles have no moving parts. The front legs are longer than the back legs in order to place the front end in deeper coals or hot ashes.

Each of the three griddles has short legs that can rest in the coals. The round part will rotate. The center griddle is enameled and grooved to catch the juices.

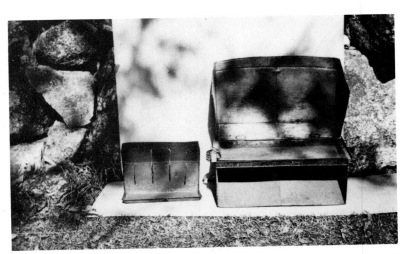

A very small tin roaster for birds, which has four hooks. The larger tin is a baking oven.

A small tin roasting oven to set before the fire with apples, potatoes or small game, and an adjustable iron toaster.

Four fireplace toasters. The back two have swivel handles for turning. The front two are on legs and the toast holder rotates on a pivot.

A roasting oven or tin kitchen with the back door open, which is used for inspection or for basting the roast. The iron spit goes through the middle of the oven and can be set at different positions.

Left to right: Two wrought iron oven peels, a salamander and a spatula.

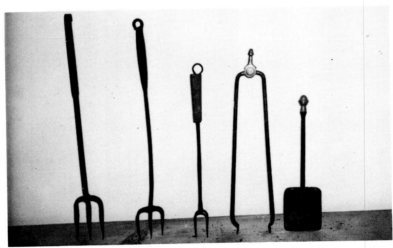

A group of small utensils, including a fork, three ladles, one of which has a brass bowl, and a spatula.

Another group of tools including three meat forks, a pair of tongs, and a spatula.

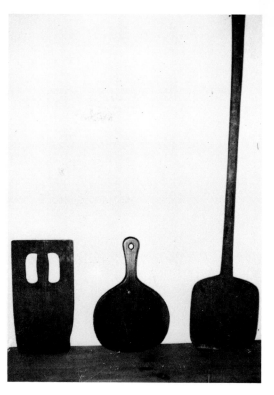

Left: A steel skewer holder and skewers. Right: A rare wrought iron skewer holder and skewers.

Two wooden spatulas at left and center. Each has a thin bottom edge and one has a unique grip for a handle. At right is a wooden oven peel.

Left to right: A brass skimmer with wrought iron handle, a spatula, shovel and hearth brush.

A variety of utensils: left to right, a skimmer used in making tallow candles, a potato basket, coffee roaster and a large pot skimmer.

A group of wrought iron oven peels, each with individual finial at the handle's top end. A wrought iron handled copper warming pan.

A brass clock or bottle jack hangs from the author's mantelpiece. The rotating wheel which hangs underneath has hooks on it. It is made of iron.

This photo shows the jack rack to better advantage. It attaches to the mantelpiece and enables the jack to slide out or in.

"Ancient" Flintlock musket and powder horn.

For the bake oven—two bean pots and a sheet iron oven door.

Fire or coals carrier, small brass toaster with telescope handle, and on the left, a metal container with copper bottom, made to stick in ashes to keep toddy hot.

Foot warmers of several shapes and sizes. The tin tray for holding coals is shown with warmer on right.

Unusual bed warmers to contain hot water. One is of heavy tin and the other, called a "pig," is of pottery.

A plate rest which hangs on a crane in the fireplace at the Governor William Greene House. The sliding part of this rest is made of brass. Owned by: Mrs. William Roelker, Jr.

A ring trivet holding a small pan; the table fire screen; and ember tongs.

An ornate brass fire screen, one of a pair owned by Mrs. William Greene Roelker, Jr. Such a screen would have been found only in the homes of the well-to-do.

A small table fire screen to shield the face, and a floor screen to shield the body from the fireplace heat. Both are adjustable for height.

A flax spinning wheel in The Bygones Museum. In the background is a loom for weaving cloth, a piece of which is on the floor underneath the wheel.

Small spinning wheel used by "brides to be" when spinning parties were held.

A flax spinning wheel of usual size and conventional type used in the Colonies. This one is in a room at the Pliny Freeman farmhouse at Old Sturbridge Village.

An unusual type of spinning wheel—a very small one also taken to spinning parties.

Unusual cresset or cupdog andirons. A crane or bar also is attached to each andiron. When swung together they make a crane rod from andiron to andiron. Utensils or other things can be hung from this rod in front of the fire. A pair of creepers are shown between the cresset andirons, which are placed backward to the viewer. Owned by Nancy Allen Holst

Small andirons, sometimes called firedogs.

A double bellows on the hearth before the author's fireplace. The only other one known by the author is at Whitehall, Bishop Berkeley's House in Portsmouth, R. I., which is illustrated here.

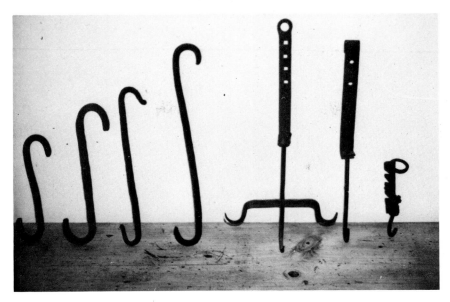

Four pot hooks of different lengths, a dangle spit or adjustable meat hooks, and two rather short trammels.

Four fine oven peels of varying lengths with the handle tips individually "stylized" by the blacksmith.

A spit bar with sliding prongs on each end to hold a roast of meat in place as it revolves in front of fireplace. Special andirons with a set of hooks or racks on the inner or outer side of the uprights hold the spit bar in place.

A brass plate warmer in the fireplace at the Governor William Greene House, home of Mrs. William Roelker, Jr. The andirons have fender posts, one of which can be seen, which substitute for creepers.

An overmantel panel painted on wood. Found in the attic of the Pope House, Spencer, Mass. Occasionally overmantel panels or fireboards were decorated with a view of the house in which they were used. Early 19th Century, now in the Tavern at Old Sturbridge Village.

Overmantel panel—oil on wood depicts the American spread eagle. Taken from over the fireplace of a house in Exeter, N. H.—1810-1830. Now in the Tavern at Old Sturbridge Village.

Fireboard—Decorated or undecorated boards like this were often placed in front of fireplaces when they were not in use. This one is supposed to have come from a house in the western part of Massachusetts, early 1800's and is now at Old Sturbridge Village.

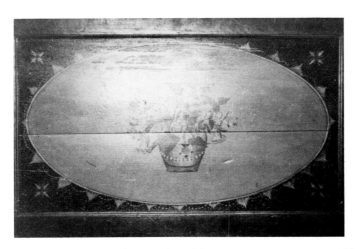

Fireboard with stencilled decoration, early 19th Century, at Tavern, Old Sturbridge Village.

Fireboard, New England scene, circa 1820, at Old Sturbridge Village.

Plate Warmer, Gen. Salem Towne House, Old Sturbridge Village.

Sad iron in front of brick oven door. Iron insert which is heated when used is shown.

Butter Churns with dashers. The end churns are made of wood. The middle one is tin.

Crane pot hooks, one of which has three racks for three positions, which is unusual.

Fireback, plate rest and three-rack pot holder are shown in author's fireplace.

A curved brass fireplace fender with a vine decoration cut in it.

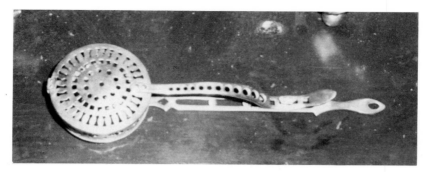

Unusual Chestnut Roaster, owned by Mr. and Mrs. Rufus Fuller of North Kingston, R. I.

Courtesy of Mrs. Lawrence M. Moore

A footman, which is a metal stand used to hold something hot before the fireplace. There are four legs, which distinguishes it from a trivet. The opening in the top is for convenience in picking it up.

Brass fireplace furnishings are found chiefly in the homes of the more well-to-do.

184

BIBLIOGRAPHY

Asburn, Burl Nelf & Wilber, Gordon Owen; *Pewter, spun, wrought & cast*. International Textbook Co., Scranton, Pa. 1938.

Beecher, Lyman, *Lyman Beecher's Autobiography*, edited by Barbara M. Cross.

Bowles, Ella Shannon, *Homespun Handicrafts*, Philadelphia: J. B. Lippincott, 1931.

Brown, Albert F., and Norman M. Isham, *Early Rhode Island Houses*. Providence: Preston and Rounds, 1895.

Carrick, Alice Van Leer, *Collectors Luck*, 1919, and *The Next to Nothing House*. Boston: Atlantic Monthly Press, 1922.

Chamberlain, Samuel, *Beyond New England Thresholds*. New York: Hastings House, 1937.

Cross, Barbara M., *Lyman Beecher's Autobiography*. Belnap Press, Harvard University, 1961.

Dearstyne, Howard, and A. Lawrence Kocher, *Colonial Williamsburg, Its Buildings and Gardens*. Scranton, Pennsylvania: Hadden Craftsmen, 1949.

Dow, George Francis, *The Arts and Crafts of New England 1704–1775*. Topsfield, Massachusetts: Wayside Press, 1927.

Downing, Antoinette Forrester, *Early Homes of Rhode Island*. Richmond, Virginia: Garret and Wassie, 1937.

Dyer, Walter A., *The Lure of the Antique*. New York: Century Co., 1910.

Earle, Alice Morse, *Home Life in Colonial Days*. New York: McMillan, 1898.

Ellis, Asa, Jun., *The Country Dyers Assistant*. Brookfield, Massachusetts: E. Merriam and Co., 1798.

French, Leigh, Jr., *Colonial Interiors*. New York: W. Helburn, Inc., 1923.

Gould, Mary Earle, *The Early American Home*. New York: Medill, McBride, 1949.

Haley, John W., *History of Rhode Island*, Vol. II, The Old Stone Bank Series.

Harriman, Walter, *The History of Warner, New Hampshire*. Concord, New Hampshire: The Republic Press Association, 1879.

Harlley, Edward Neal, *Ironworks on the Saugus*, Norman, Oklahoma, University of Oklahoma Press, 1957.

Hough, Walter, *Heating and Lighting Utensils, in the United States National Museums*, Bulletin 141. Washington, D. C.: Smithsonian Institution, Government Printing Office, 1928.

Isham, Norman M., and Albert F. Brown, *Early Rhode Island Houses*. Providence: Preston and Rounds, 1895.

Isham, Norman M., Glossary of Colonial Architectural Terms.

Jekyll, Gertrude, and Sidney Jones, *Old English Household Life*. New York and London: Charles Scribner's Sons, 1939.

Jones, Sidney, and Gertrude Jekyll, *Old English Household Life*. New York and London: Charles Scribner's Sons, 1939.

Kaufman, Henry J., *Early American Ironware: Cast and Wrought*. Rutland, Vermont: Charles E. Tuttle, 1966.

Kocher, A. Lawrence, and Howard Dearstyne, *Colonial Williamsburg, Its Buildings and Gardens*. Scranton, Pennsylvania: Hadden Craftsmen, 1949.

Lachlan, Carli, *The Candle Book*. New York: M. Barrows, 1956.

Ladd, Paul Revere, *Windmill Cottage and Longfellow in Rhode Island History*. Rhode Island Historical Society, January 1967.

Lindsay, J. Seymour, *Iron and Brass Implements of the English and American Home*. London Medici Society, 1927.

Longfellow, Henry W., *The Hanging of the Crane*. Boston: Houghton Mifflin Co., 1881.

Longfellow, Henry W., *Complete Poetical Works*. Boston: Houghton Mifflin Co., 1883.

McClinton, Katherine Morrison, *Antique Collecting for Everyone*. Bonanza Books, 1951.

Morley, Christopher, "Chimney Smoke", George H. Deran Co. N.Y. 1921.

Mount Vernon Ladies Association of the Union, *Handbook of Mount Vernon*. Judd and Detweiler, Inc.

Nutting, Wallace, *Early American Iron Works*. Wallace Nutting, Inc.

Nutting, Wallace, *Furniture Treasury, Vol. II, Furniture of the Pilgrim Century*. New York: MacMillan, 1948.

Peirce, Josephine H., *Fire on the Hearth*. Springfield, Massachusetts: Pond-Ekberg Co., 1951.

Putnam, J. Pickering, *The Open Fireplace in All Ages*. Boston: James R. Osgood Co., 1882.

Rawson, Marion Nicholl, *The Earth Earthy*. New York: E. P. Dutton Co., 1937.

Rawson, Marion Nicholl, *Candle Days*. New York: Appleton-Century, 1927.

Robacher, Earl F., *Pennsylvania Dutch Stuff*. Philadelphia: University of Pennsylvania Press, 1944.

Robinson, W., *Wood Fires for the Country House*. England: Mayflower Press

Roy, L. M. A., *The Candle Book*. Brattleboro, Vermont: Stephen Daye Press, 1938.

Shuffrey, L. A., *The English Fireplace and Its Accessories*. London: B. T. Batsford

Sloane, Eric, *The Seasons of America Past*. New York, N. Y.: Wilfred Funk, Inc., 1958.

Smith, Helen Evertson, *Colonial Days and Ways*. New York: The Century Co., 1900.

Sonn, Albert A., *Early American Wrought Iron, Vol. II*. New York and London: Charles Scribner Sons, 1928.

Stowe, Harriet Beecher, *Old Fireside Stories*, Chapter XXXVII. Boston: Houghton Mifflin, 1899.

Swank, James N., *The Manufacture of Iron in New England*, edited by William T. Davis. Boston: D. H. Hurd and Co.

Sweeney, John A. H., *Treasure House of Early American Rooms of Henry duPont: Winterthur Museum*. Viking Press, 1963.

Thorn, C. Jordan, Silver and Pewtermarks; Tudor Publishing Co., N. Y., 1949.

Tunis, Edwin, *Colonial Living*. Cleveland: World Publishing Co., 1957.

Watson, Aldren A., *The Village Blacksmith*. New York: Thomas Y. Crowell Co.

Whittier, John Greenleaf, *Snowbound and Other Poems*. Cambridge, Massachusetts: Houghton Mifflin, 1944.

INDEX